CATS

"John Rush writes about the diverse array of cat realms from a place of delightful passion and knowledge. One can never quite see cats the same way after reading this book. He weaves together mythology and science, history and spirituality, and cosmic and pop culture in order to aid the mass consciousness. Everyone who cares about drawing into complete harmony with the strength of a feline's essence—or any living creature—should own a copy of *Cats: Keepers of the Spirit World.*"

RUSLANA REMENNIKOVA, ANIMAL INTUIT,
WRITER, AND SOUND ALCHEMIST

"Shamanic shapeshifters of human consciousness—these wondrous four-legged demi-gods weave in and out of the astral plane influencing evolutionary growth on levels humans have yet to comprehend. Cats are the gatekeepers into our unconscious world, capable of entering into dimensions to impart magic and healing medicine in those spaces where wounds hide. They carry the secrets of the universe within their souls; lineages of many worlds rooted in tradition pass through them and onto their human caretakers. Their distinct meow is heard by every angel, as they walk through their existence embodying love and hope. They absorb darkness so that our light can shine over and over again and ask for nothing in return. May we honor them with the respect they truly deserve."

LAURA AVERSANO, AUTHOR OF
AFFIRMATIONS OF THE LIGHT IN TIMES OF DARKNESS

CATS

KEEPERS
of the
SPIRIT WORLD

A Sacred Planet Book

John A. Rush

Destiny Books
Rochester, Vermont

Destiny Books
One Park Street
Rochester, Vermont 05767
www.DestinyBooks.com

Destiny Books is a division of Inner Traditions International

Sacred Planet Books are curated by Richard Grossinger, Inner Traditions editorial board member and cofounder and former publisher of North Atlantic Books. The Sacred Planet collection, published under the umbrella of the Inner Traditions family of imprints, includes works on the themes of consciousness, cosmology, alternative medicine, dreams, climate, permaculture, alchemy, shamanic studies, oracles, astrology, crystals, hyperobjects, locutions, and subtle bodies.

Cataloging-in-Publication Data for this title is available from the Library of Congress

ISBN 978-1-64411-746-0 (print)
ISBN 978-1-64411-747-7 (ebook)

Printed and bound in the United States by Lake Book Manufacturing, LLC

10 9 8 7 6 5 4 3 2 1

Text design and layout by Kenleigh Manseau
This book was typeset in Garamond Premier Pro with Gill Sans and Grand Cru used as display typefaces

To send correspondence to the author of this book, mail a first-class letter to the author c/o Inner Traditions • Bear & Company, One Park Street, Rochester, VT 05767, and we will forward the communication, or contact the author directly at **jarush43@gmail.com** or **www.clinicalanthropology.com**.

Contents

Preface

There is more to life than we experience with our senses, with some individuals capable of sensing beyond the known human sense modalities. Cats and humans share certain senses, but cat senses are more finely tuned, perfectly appropriate for a predator. Cats also have capabilities we don't possess, as well as senses that we might (or might not) possess, which are "turned on" in the cat.

Moreover, there may be other dimensions; there is nothing in quantum mechanics that prohibits other dimensions, wormholes, and so on that may be detectable by cats—as well as some humans. It is the cat's physical abilities and sensory capabilities or characteristics, real in some cases and perhaps imagined in others, that we interpret as spiritual. In fact, in many ways the cat is a mirror of us—mysterious, magical, loving, reverent, powerful, revengeful, and distant. Why do cats and humans seem to complement each other?

Modern humans and our ancient, ancient ancestors have a deep history with predators. Modern cats, as we know them, show up, not coincidently, at the same time as recognizable predecessors to our kind, between twenty and thirty million years ago. Have you ever been afraid of the dark? For our ancient ancestors, they had every right to fear the dark as most cats are night predators. As the reader will see, organisms program and reprogram their DNA in anticipation of the next

generation, and one of the mechanisms for programming and repro-
gramming is intense *stress*—the fear of being eaten, for example—and
we have etched this fear onto our genes. This did not happen accidentally or randomly. Recall all the stories and myths involving cannibal-
istic monsters, such as Baba Yaga and Lilith (sometimes configured as
a cat), that excite our imagination. But for our ancestors the monsters
were real: predators (mainly cats) are animals that could get you on the
ground or in the trees while you slept. And demonstrated in the pages
to follow, this fear etched on our genes is a starting point from which
we can appreciate our connection to cats as well as their (and our) spiritual nature.

I wish to thank the staff at Inner Traditions for the preparation
of this manuscript, as well as my wife, Katie, for her observations and
insights that helped made this project possible. And, of course, I thank
our feline friends who, over the many years, have provided companionship and insights into not only cat behavior but human behavior as well.

1

Sleeping Kittens, Crouching Tigers

Cats—a mystery. They are like no other animal. Unlike dogs, sheep, goats, cattle, horses, and any other domesticated animal, they aren't beasts of burden, they don't produce milk for cheese or yogurt or eggs, they don't sniff out drugs, and they aren't food stuff, at least in most cultures under normal circumstances, although there are a couple of exceptions noted in the pages to follow. So why do we keep them around? Moreover we have (at least in our household) become their servants. We feed them, provide shelter, clean up their cat boxes, brush them and vacuum up the massive amounts of hair they shed, clean up when they spray (which is rare) and vomit (which is more frequent), make sure they are hugged and loved, spend very large sums of money on veterinarian visits, and we do this with a smile on our face and a song in our heart. The explanation for this—what might be considered irrational behavior—exists deep in time, back with our earliest, earliest ancestors. For as long as primates have been on planet Earth there have been cats and their ancestors. We have evolved together, and this is where we find the origins of not only our servitude to cats, but of their spiritual nature as well.

This book is about origins, human and cat, for it is by looking at our ancient past that we can identify our deep connections to cats and our eventual attachment of spiritual characteristics to them. As the reader will come to recognize, the spiritual nature of cats in many ways reflects ourselves, an echo that emerged over fifty-five million years ago.

CONNECTING TO CATS

I am a biological anthropologist and symbologist, and my interest in cats began many years ago as I was attempting to understand our evolutionary origins, which, by the way, are sketchy at best. One of the reasons for this is lack of data, the bones, which are few and far between. There are very, very large gaps in our knowledge. Our ancestral relationships are, for the most part, guesswork, which oftentimes ends up in biological anthropology text books as truth. We create models, present them in books and articles—a commitment of sorts—and come to believe them, often holding up our understanding for many decades. This is not a criticism so much as the acknowledgment that we need stability in our thinking; anchor points, if you will, to help us explain our experiences. It is dangerous to alter a person's reality too rapidly because, by doing so, you risk psychosis. So we, for psychological protection, get stuck in our models of the world. "Scientific" narratives, once published in prestigious books and journals, are difficult to abandon. "So it is written, so it shall be."

Cats are apex predators and our ancient ancestors, emerging in the Oligocene (thirty-four to twenty-three million years ago) and Miocene (twenty-three to six million years ago), were prey animals for millions of years. In more recent times—that is, for our ancestors of between three million and eight hundred thousand years ago in various areas of the African continent and areas outside Africa—our relationship to the numerous carnivores and scavengers gradually changed. We learned how to scavenge carcasses left by the cats (and other predators) out of necessity when our normal foods (fruits, berries, and tubers, for instance) were in short supply; we are in debt to these animals. Now surrounded by miniature versions of these powerful felines, my wife and I began a long-term study of their behavioral patterns.

We manage a feral cat community, currently about fifteen or more cats. Because feral cats are mobile we are definitely visited by strays, especially at night. Presently there are about five ferals who come through our property and stay for various lengths of time. If they are accepted by the community—usually if they are young and subservient but persistent—they can become long-term members. We began trapping the ferals many years ago, so now it is rare to have really young cats come onto the property. We have one very young black longhair who has bonded with two of the cats and seems to be winning over the two bullies in the group, Stimpy and Timmy. The older the cat, the lower the probability he or she will be accepted by the community. The reasons for this are independence (cats are not a small-group animal like a dog) and dominance.

We also permit nine felines to share our household. This inside/outside arrangement has allowed a more intimate relationship and observation of cat behavior. Over the course of thirty-five years we have been able to identify features of the cat considered spiritual by our ancestors, for example, the ancient Sumerians, Egyptians, and North and South Americans. The reader, however, will be surprised to read that cats as such were not worshipped, although certain *characteristics,* considered otherworldly, became associated with different gods and goddesses. Before continuing, however, I need to define terms often used when discussing cats.

DEFINING WORSHIP, SPIRIT, SPIRITUAL, AND SACRED

The word "spiritual" is thrown about in reference to people, places, and things, and in order to understand what I'm referring to when used with respect to cats, I need to consider the various uses of this and other related terms.

First, there is spirit as an *entity*, a god or demon lurking in the dark; spirits can also inhabit people, places, and things, such as with demonic possession, a Tibetan temple, or a tree, as would be the case for Indigenous peoples living in the northeast United States. The Seneca, for example, would find a tree, often basswood, make an offering of tobacco along with ritual prayer, and then carve a face into the tree, thus releasing its spirit. The spirit would then be captured in the form of a medicine mask, used for healing. Some of these masks are quite similar with the big difference being the shape of the mouth, as it is through the mouth that a particular spirit speaks in order to cure or curse people. Some of these masks are quite old, and the older the mask the more power it contains. The analogy here is that with age comes wisdom (in most cases), and this sentiment becomes attached to the mask. These masks are usually in the care of shamans.

Spirit entities are otherworldly beings thought to interact with humans in both positive and negative ways. We also use the word spirit for an animal or person's life force that leaves the body during illness, trance, near death experiences, and at death. There may be some validity to this idea of a "life force," one's soul, that leaves the body. Shamans are said to be able to control this energy, leave their body, and fly, often with the help of mind-altering substances.

Second, "spirit" can also relate to an attitude or psychological state, as to be in "good spirits" or to have "Christmas spirit," which, in some cases, also alludes to being possessed by good entities.

And then there are the "spirits" one purchases at the liquor store, like "demon rum." This connection actually comes from Arab alchemists who, when collecting vapors during distillation, considered the vapor as the "spirit" of the material being processed or distilled.

Third, spiritual (a characteristic), as related to a person's personality or soul, is a nonmaterial aspect of the human animal, and other animals as well. Then there is the religious cleric, a "spiritual leader" who looks after that nonmaterial part of us, like the "life force" mentioned earlier. There is also "spiritual music," for example, Gospel music sung in church or revival meetings designed to appeal to our otherworldly nature. Music is very important in many religious traditions as it can act as a medium for contacting that other world through what is called an altered state of consciousness (which is really awareness). One feature of music is the octave (this is a time or space between ascending or descending tones). Octave theory, the esoteric cosmology taught by G. I. Gurdjieff (1973) as well as Gadalla (2002, 2018), suggests the universe was built on harmonic balance, anticipated in the seven chakras in Hinduism, the Kabala in Judaism, the World Tree or the Christian cross, the axis mundi around which the universe turns—basically that all the secrets of the universe are connected through harmonics.

Fourth, spirituality, in some ways is like spirit in that it is conceptualized as something that one searches for in oneself, others, or the universe. Spirituality is considered a good thing, but a "good thing" can be defined in many ways. Martyrdom and murder in the name of a god, for example, might be considered a way to connect with something larger than oneself (Perlmutter 2004; Juergensmeyer 2003; Firestone 1999).

Sacred refers to that which is connected to otherworldly matters. The opposite would be secular. However, in my definition, a sacred animal refers to the animal's *characteristics* that are interpreted as otherworldly or not possessed by the human animal; it is *not that the animal is or was necessarily worshipped*. Closely related to sacred is the word "holy."

The word "worship" is often used to characterize our relationship to cats, and this needs further clarification. Worship, as anthropologists define the term, involves supplication, begging, and actual servitude to a deity. In Judaism (Yahweh), Christianity (God the Father or Yahweh), and Islam (Allah), one is a slave to the deity, following His instructions to the letter—"or else!" These three deities are not only father figures but, as outlined in a former publication, they are demonic in character (Rush 2023).

Identity with the divine as in polytheistic traditions, rather than servitude, is another issue altogether. With identity you can *become* the divine—"I and the Father are One." You can never be God in mono-theistic traditions. When most researchers say animal worship, they are really referring to *identity with the animal* and its perceived other-worldly behaviors or characteristics. As the reader will see, using the above definition, animal worship is quite rare.

Veneration is another term used in connection with the spiritual, but it refers to respect or dedication to gods and goddesses, as well as to cats and humans. We will return to these terms as well as explore others throughout the book.

ANIMALS AS SYMBOLS OF NATURE, BOTH GOOD AND EVIL

We speak in metaphor. We often refer to nature; for example, to be as "strong as an ox" or that we all have our "mountains to climb." These statements are not to be taken literally. We use characteristics of nature when describing our world, such as "a rosy colored sunset." Then there is "the lights are on and no one's home" or to be "half a bubble off plumb." These are what we might call urban metaphors, as they are connected to a different technology not available to our ancestors until more recent times. In order to make such analogies we need experience with colors in nature, animal behavior, and technological sophistication as reference points, especially if we are to share our experiences with others. We describe people as animals, for example, "He's a rat" (or dog) or "She's catty," with each having a reference to some characteristics of animal behavior or, perhaps, insects or plants, that is, to be like a "little gnat" or "dumb as a turnip" (although turnips are pretty smart in their own world). They are ways of describing one's experience and telling colorful stories; such descriptions help us more clearly share our experiences because, again, they act as general reference points.

The terms *spirit, spiritual,* and *spirituality,* however, refer to a different plane of existence, something we are possessed by or with, or that comes from another dimension, or perhaps a special part of us that leaves the body during out-of-body travel, near death experiences, or death. It is also that which lies hidden, although we know it is there. Many scientists and academics profess that there is nothing beyond what we experience or what can be measured in material science, although many others have doubts, recognizing that there is more to our existence than that which we can measure (Davies 1983, 2008; Grossinger 2022).

Forces of nature, especially for our ancient ancestors, were often considered "otherworldly" or controlled by otherworldly powers, specifically those not understood—for example, why it rains, where lightening comes from, and the power of animals. This lack of understanding turns into what we call magical thinking when describing our experiences and their causes. These narratives are constructed because the mind does not like mysteries, and mysteries can be solved with a story or a myth, for psychological protection, if you will, that aids in our survival.

Worship, again, has to do with ritual process and obedience or following a directive issued by a divine presence and delivered through the deity's messengers: the priest, rabbi, or imam. On the other side, as mentioned above, is the concept of *identity with* the divine and actually becoming the divine. For worship, at least in my definition, there is a barrier between you and the divine where you ask for favors, mainly to satisfy your animal nature (life/health, progeny, and economic security of some type that maintains the other two).

In the early Christian cults, the participant could identify with and become (commune with) Jesus. Jesus, at least in my analysis and the conclusions of others, was an experience obtained by consuming the *Amanita muscaria* mushroom and the ritual processes surrounding its consumption. After 325 CE this was converted into a religion of worship where Jesus had to become a real person so he could suffer, become a martyr, and die for our sins. After 325 CE you could no longer be God/Jesus, only a follower or adherent with faith (Rush 2022).

The word *divine* is often used to describe cats and other animals (Ikram 2014). The word divine can relate, as an adjective, to a deity, a place, or a characteristic a person or other animal might possess. Being forgiving is often considered a divine characteristic. Perceived beauty in nature could be considered divine. Cats, however, are not divine animals, but they have *characteristics* that could place them in that category—such as purring or their acute sense of hearing. They may act as an early warning system, as guardians for temple priests or for workers in the field who have to contend with scorpions and snakes. The question becomes, if cats are divine, are the monster cats divine as well? I suppose that if you consider monsters otherworldly then you have a case for divine, but it is unlikely that most people, except perhaps a satanist, would describe monsters using that terminology.

In review, there is a claim by many that specific animals connected to various cultures were worshipped, but animal worship is rare and it is *identity* with an animal's characteristics that these authors are pointing to. In my opinion, there is nothing divine or spiritual in worshipping a god to whom you are enslaved (Yahweh, God the Father, or Allah). *Identification with* various animals is what brings out our spiritual nature.

2

Cat Evolution

A more complete discussion of evolutionary processes is available in *What Darwin and Dawkins Didn't Know* (2020) and *Endocellular Selection* (2021b); cat evolution is specifically presented in *Cat Tales: Origins, Interactions, and Domestication of Felis catus* (2021a). It is important here to note that Darwin was absolutely, positively wrong regarding the processes of evolution and the origin of species. His position, as it has continued to this day, is that the universe and the life within it came about randomly and accidentally. Some say the universe came out of nothing and then randomly self-assembled (Krauss 2013), but equilibrium thermodynamics does not allow molecular self-assembly as speculated by Krauss (Rush 2021b, 85–86). By assuming that life came about randomly, Darwin (and the Neo-Darwinians) could eliminate any notion of an intelligent universe *and* spirituality of any kind; according to Darwin and his followers, all that you experience, past and present, can be studied and understood using mathematics, chemistry, and classical physics; they have great faith in their position.

Some scientists, however, have bypassed Darwin, realizing there are many things materialistic science cannot explain. How the brain works, for example, is an enigma. Although the brain is made up of particles (chemicals, tissue types, fluids), we *think* in waveforms. Where do waves come from, how are they produced? We can measure them but we lack an understanding of their cause. Interestingly enough, the universe is based on a waveform, which materializes when observed, measured, or experienced by a lifeform. How the waveform materializes is determined by the nervous system of the plant, insect, or animal having the experience. What is the origin of this waveform that is the universe? No one knows, although some physicists and biologists claim they do (Krauss 2013; Dawkins 2019). In order to have what we call a universe there has to be a code or energy that precedes it. No one, to my knowledge, can prove the negative, that no coding preceded the origin of the universe. I will return to the quantum level, waveforms, and spirituality in chapter 7.

THE MYTH OF RANDOM MUTATIONS AND LIFE WITHOUT PURPOSE

Darwin's ideas, still dogmatically adhered to by many, are as follows: random mutations (by chance, accidental, unsystematic, and unintentional) which produced DNA and the multitude of chemicals and enzymes necessary for functionality, plus natural selection (culling out the unfit), plus time, equals new species; that is, Random Mutations + Natural Selection + Time = New Species. This process has never been verified using the materialistic model the Darwinians claim to support. I challenge anyone in the scientific community to show me proof that their model has been scientifically proven correct. What we do have are anecdotal statements about *outcomes* rather than the causes of outcomes. There is no science (math, physics, or chemistry) informing how random events create functional codes.

Here is what we really know *scientifically*: random events do not create *functional* codes; DNA, for example, is a *potentially* functional code. Yes, a computer programmer can create a program to produce random numbers in such a way as to produce a sort of code (no *functional codes*, codes that contain usable information in a system of codes, have ever been created this way), *but this is researcher (intelligence) interference.* In other words, an intelligence (the researcher) is creating the coding that creates the random code. So, when you remove this interference, random events cannot produce a functional code. But there is more.

In fact, even to randomly create a very small *functioning* protein (one that will fold up properly and then be used in some manner), say with fifty amino acids (the building blocks of DNA), would take longer than the age of the universe (Rush 2020). In order for a protein to be functional it has to fold properly, which means all the nucleotides and amino acids have to line up properly like teeth in a gear mechanism, thus adding much of the complexity to this molecule. Without proper folding there can be no storage of information, and therefore the molecule is not usable. What we are dealing with is this: flip fifty coins in the air, individually, and have them *all* come up heads or *all* tails. The probability of that happening just once in your lifetime, even if you were flipping coins every second, comes pretty close to impossible (though miracles do happen). Actually, it is much more complex because instead of dealing with just two variables (heads or tails), with DNA you are juggling four nucleotides (adenine, guanine, thymine, cytosine) that build the amino acids, and everything has to match up perfectly. Right away you can see that random events are not specific enough to create a functioning system. Also, in order to make a functional protein you need a plan, so there is even a larger problem here.

Initially, at the beginning of the universe, when enough cooling had occurred so organic (carbon-based) chemicals could form, why create a functioning protein? What would be its function or purpose? *Codes, in order to be functional, have to articulate with other codes as a unit,* and that unit would have to be goal oriented. For a code to be useful it has to have something to do. Where would such an orientation or purpose come from? The reason why serviceable codes cannot be created randomly is simple: they require direction or purpose, and this requires intelligence and a goal. As mentioned above, *a useful code would have to be part of a functioning system. The term functional cannot be used outside of a system with parts,* and that would require numerous proteins (enzymes, etc.) not just one (Behe 1996, 2007). For a living system to exist past one generation it has to replicate itself, and a single protein cannot replicate itself. DNA cannot, as far as I am aware, replicate itself without the help of other enzymes. But first, certainly, you would have to build a protein, and random is not going to accomplish this. For a *system* like a bacterium to come about randomly and all at once (a bacterium cannot be constructed piecemeal) and with all the necessary functional proteins is highly improbable if not impossible. In order to prove their position, the Darwinians have to show purpose. You just don't make a fender for a car unless you already have a car in mind. Likewise, a telephone number would be meaningless without a telephone system already in place. Yes, miracles do happen. Darwin's ideas have held up our understanding of the origin of species for over 160 years! We can do better than this.

THE MYTH OF NATURAL SELECTION

Next is natural selection. In a phrase, this is survival of the fittest. That is to say the most fit are the ones who are more likely to pass on their genetic material. This sounds like a good idea, until we run it in reverse—survival of the fittest, it is the fit who survive. Natural selection is a circular argument and is meaningless. Are the ones that survive the most fit or just lucky? What do the Darwinians mean by "fit?" *"Fit" has never been defined in any meaningful way.* Moreover, nature, if we are to believe the Darwinians on this point, selects by chance. If mutations are random, then natural selection has to be random as well. If evolution is all random you would never be able to fine-tune any system, for example, a shoulder joint for accurate throwing or bipedalism and a foot for not only walking but running, too. Natural selection cannot pick and choose specific traits or target only a specific part or parts of the genetic code. Further, most biological systems evolve in a *mosaic* fashion. In other words, you will not encounter a bowl-shaped pelvis like ours without at the same time providing a knee joint that locks out and a bipedal foot (and probably an "S" shaped spine). These "parts" did not evolve independently, as many anthropologists continue to believe. Just think of the complexity connected to bipedalism that would, according to the Darwinians, emerge randomly. This is highly unlikely, although, again, miracles do happen—but then you are left with explaining the miracle. (A bowl-shaped pelvis, by the way, is of no use to a quadruped.)

We hear that bursts of cosmic rays possibly altered the genetic code of our ancestors, producing new species, us included. Again, this sounds like a good idea, until you realize that any alterations would be random; there is no specificity in random mutations. In fact, such mutations, if not corrected, usually lead to disease and death; random mutations *devolve* life. If natural selection really did select for fitness, why are there so many genetic diseases? And we can't blame this all on pollution and carcinogens, for many genetic disease issues came about thousands if not millions of years ago. Ice Man, for example, dated to circa 3500 BCE, had a genetic predisposition to heart disease, supposedly a modern issue connected to diet (Geggel 2018). After 3.5 billion years we should all be perfect if natural selection actually selected for the "fittest"; further evolution is unnecessary.

For Darwin and his followers, they have great *faith* in their position even without scientific proof. This is no different from having faith that a god or energy of some type created the universe. Both positions fit into the category of metaphysics. We have to look past Darwin and his atheist followers. Here is a question: Is having faith in the nonexistence of something a spiritual act?

ENDOCELLULAR SELECTION:
DECISION-MAKING AND PURPOSEFUL EVOLUTION

We know that life changes or evolves, but the direction of this change is not toward any type of ultimate perfection as there is no way of knowing what that should be. Change is *purposely prompted by the cell,* by the organism, in *anticipation of environmental conditions for the next generation.* And sometimes the cells get it wrong because they cannot predict the future, only anticipate it in terms of what cells are experiencing during gestation and after parturition; they cannot anticipate catastrophic events. We cannot predict the future either, and this is one reason we rely on divination techniques of one type or another.

The elimination of dinosaurs around sixty-five million years ago led to a proliferation of mammals including cats and our human ancestors. How did this come about? Research over the past two decades reveals that the cell itself is making changes to the DNA.* This is especially the case during gestation as the cells are reacting to the mother's *stressors* (like cold, heat, nutritional scarcity, fear reactions or predator stress, and illness). *Such stressors affect groups and not just singular individuals.* These reactions and consequent genetic alterations are employed in *anticipation* of the world to come or conditions after parturition. For example, if the mother was malnourished during the first trimester, the cells make alterations in anticipation of a meager food supply. Cells, as mentioned, can get it wrong however, and for example anticipate a meager food supply but instead encounter a rich food environment. This can lead to overindulgence and type 2 diabetes (Rush 2020, 2021a, 2021b). This can occur on an individual as well as group level. This cellular behavior—that is, altering the genetic code—is called *epigenetics* and, in a larger sense, *endocellular selection, wherein the organism is evolving itself.* In short, the cat, just like

---

*See Lieff 2020 for references to recent research.

humans and all other life forms, alters its DNA as it responds to environmental stressors. Random mutations certainly occur, but they are corrected in most cases, and when not corrected will usually lead to disease states of various severity. Your body, for example, is a *system* of cells, tissues, and organs, and when one coding is altered randomly (mutation) it can have a cascading effect on the rest of the cells and tissues. When *your cells* alter their DNA, they alter *all* the other parts and pathways necessary for proper functioning—usually. When the medical community learns how to do this we will literally control life and death; this ability is years away.

Once we consider (or rather admit) that cells think, make decisions, and alter their genetic coding accordingly, we can see how when influenced by the *same* stressor (predator, nutrition, cold, heat), group members alter the *same* genetic coding sequences—we see this in the Dutch Hunger Winter studies (Rush 2020, 62–66) and rats (Marchlewicz et al. 2020, 7). The alterations, then, that might lead to adaptation in the future are part of the *group* genome, so it doesn't matter who mates with whom or whether an individual is removed from the "gene pool" prior to procreating—the changes to the coding sequence(s) will go marching on. In this case the external stressors (Nature) select nothing and have little to do with selecting for fitness; stressors only offer possibilities, adversities to which the cell adapts (Rush 2021b, 110).

Again it is the organism that is altering its genetic code; it is the organism that is selecting and adapting and not simply at the mercy of what Nature throws at it. Darwinism has only maintained prominence in the academic community for political reasons, and when politics invades science, the science can no longer be trusted because it is no longer objective. We've been with Darwin now for over 160 years, and his opinions have been unproductive. The reason for this is the Darwinian's inability to explain *how* random mutations or natural selection produce new species. Saying random mutations lead to new species is an outcome, not an explanation of how the codes are produced randomly. Darwinism is the greatest hoax ever perpetrated and maintained by the scientific and academic communities.

I also need to add the process of symbiosis, acquiring new genetic information from bacteria and viruses, as an extremely important issue in the origin of new species (Rush 2020). Symbiosis occurs when, for example, a virus can bypass the immune system and use mammal DNA to replicate itself and actually add to or modify the genetic coding of the host—permanently. Cats, humans, and all modern mammals (Eutheria) have a placenta designed to house and feed the fetus internally, as opposed to marsupials (opossums, kangaroos, and others in the subclass Theria), which do these tasks externally, in a pouch. The coding for our placenta was apparently acquired from a virus somewhere between eighty and a hundred million years ago, and this change happened rapidly, perhaps in a few generations (Rush 2020, 2021b). This was not a random act for the virus, any more than the development of new strains of COVID-19 are random. As I have stated in previous works, the virus, like all living things, wants immortality; this is called "will to life" (Rush 2020, 2021b). Waiting around for some random, spontaneous event to aid in survival is a death sentence; life has to be actively involved it its own evolution.

Another type of rapid evolution occurs with hybridization or the interbreeding of similar species isolated for many thousands of years. The offspring gain from the diversity of genetic material obtained from each parent. *Felis catus* is a product of such hybridization.

Epigenetics and endocellular selection are new concepts, along with symbiosis and hybridization, that offer a *scientifically verifiable* explanation of genetic processes and evolution and offer a clue as to why, as mentioned in the preface, modern cats show up during the same time period as our first identifiable ancestors, the monkeys and apes. This also helps answer the question of why cats, like sharks, have changed little over millions of years. The cat, like the shark, evolved to "perfection" in terms of obtaining calories for procreation. Our ancestral line chose intelligence and social learning as major survival mechanisms for obtaining calories, while the cat chose power, speed, stealth, sensory systems designed to locate, target, and kill, and fecundity or the ability to produce lots of its kind in a short period of time. This did not occur randomly or accidentally for us or the cats. Our ancestors had to adapt to these cat characteristics just as the cats had to adapt to our adaptations, or characteristics—the *original* battle, a genetic battle, between good and evil. Evil, in a large sense for those ancient ancestors, was the fear of being eaten, a fear we are reminded of in our children's bedtime stories.

CAT EVOLUTION AND OUR HUMAN ANCESTORS

Our understanding of the spiritual nature of cats emerged from our observation of them over the course of many millions of years. Beginning in the Cambrian time period (around 541–485 million years ago) we encounter a proliferation of life forms, most without precedent (which has never been explained by the Darwinians), and we also see recognizable predators or life eating life on a larger scale. Prior to this time, we see life-fulfilling nutrient demands through the consumption of minerals and organic materials in what has been called the "primordial soup," and certainly bacteria consuming other bacteria and viruses invading bacteria and becoming part of their genetic coding—which may be a clue to the proliferation of animals, seemingly out of nowhere, in the Cambrian. With the Cambrian we encounter predators with which we are more familiar, although many are unusual, and from the beginning of life forms on this planet (circa 3.5 billion years ago) there have been other life forms using them for food or using their genetic codes to further their own existence. We might just be food for predator space aliens; be careful whom you invite to dinner.

Our earliest ancestors of fifty-five million years ago, although not recognizable as such, were more like tree-dwelling, weasel-like critters;

nor would we recognize any cats. But there were predators, both tree and ground dwelling (Rush 2021a). There is what's called a "will to life," a programming designed to protect from injury (automatic reflexes, for example). Now think about those ancient ancestors of ours having to contend with predators who could climb trees, especially at night. The stress generated certainly would affect the *whole* group and lead to alterations in the genetic coding and the selection of physical and behavioral traits that had survival value in that environment. Group living, for example, has survival value in that we watch each other's back, as do communication strategies and calls—initially hoots and howls—that alert to danger at a distance. Life expectancy increases as the distance between you and the predator increases. The stress and fear our ancestors felt drove our evolution, and it is this fear that connects us to cats then as now. But even with these strategies no one is totally safe. Remember epigenetics and endocellular selection mentioned above—alterations of the genetic coding are a continual process leading, over time, to the species (both human and cat) we see today.

What I find most interesting, as mentioned above, is that the cats we recognize as cats and monkeys and apes show up at the same time periods during the Oligocene (thirty-four to twenty-three million years ago) and Miocene (twenty-three to six million years ago). The point is we evolved together and we needed each other, keeping in mind that the cats were the hunters and our ancestors were the food. Obviously our ancestors did not go for brawn—that is power, stealth, and so on—so it was a matter of staying alert, enhanced awareness of our surroundings, and communication strategies that led to our survival, at least to this point.

A CHANGE IN BELIEFS

There is a twist in the story that understandably had a great psychological impact on our ancestors. Around 3 to 3.4 million years ago some of our ancestors began to make stone tools (California Academy of Sciences, "Evidence of Stone Tool Use") and the question is, "Why?" Our ancestors were, for the most part, vegetarians, eating fruits, leafy vegetables, tubers, berries, and insects such as termites. Stone tools would not be needed for harvesting any of these foodstuffs; tubers can be more easily dug out of the ground, or termites out of a termite mound, with an antler pick. It appears that periods of drought and more intense seasonal changes altered the availability of foods, and it is at these times we see what I've termed *analogous thinking* coming into play (Rush 1996, 2021b). Our awareness at that time allowed us to step back from nature, take ideas from nature, and press them back in to service.

So what are stone tools? They are analogous to the teeth of the predators. With this type of thinking we began to imitate other animals, the scavengers, and it is during those times when food was in short supply that we encounter scavenging behavior. We are not genetically equipped with weapons, such as long canines and sharp claws, so we had to "borrow" them from the predators—these are the stone tools for processing carcasses left by the larger predators. So now—and this is important—not only are the cats eating our ancestors, but they are also leaving us food in our time of need. This is sort of a "giving back" by the predators—the sacrifice, if you will, practiced by many religions either directly (human or animal sacrifice) or through symbolic human sacrifice as in communion in the Catholic Mass, a deal struck in heaven.

It is at this time, around three million years ago, that we begin a different life and death relationship with cats: they leave us food, but they will eat us when the opportunity arises. We can anticipate an ambivalence toward predators because now they are not simply monsters; they are necessary threats to life and limb—that is, good and evil. Many gods show this duality of good and evil just as nature in general has a good side and a bad side.

Around eight to five hundred thousand years ago the thrusting spear comes into play and, more importantly, the throwing spear (a tooth that leaps upon its prey) is invented, making the human animal a top predator. This would cause another psychological issue, that is, a closer identity with the predators: we are them and they are us. Certainly by this time period and probably dating back three million years, we had a sophisticated language for storing information and organizing our worlds, and it is likely we named ourselves according to the powers we perceived in nature, and most certainly the animals. These would eventually become clan names: the bear, the lion, and so on.

Humans are a small-group animal. We hunted and gathered food within territories, and our populations were limited by the food available. Most of the hunter-gatherer groups numbered perhaps twenty-five to sixty members, although at specific times of the year or for special purposes larger groups might come together as evidenced at Göbekli Tepe in Turkey, dated to around twelve thousand years ago; such gatherings might have been a driving factor for the development of sedentary agriculture that occurred gradually over the course of several thousand years in the Middle East. It should be noted that animal husbandry begins about the same time as sedentary agriculture, if not earlier.

Agriculture brings about unanticipated problems, like not being able to supply all the nutritional needs for the individual, seeing that the number of plant sources became restricted. We created and had to adjust to new foods such as milk, bread, and beer. Living in close contact with animals also brought unexpected issues of disease and pests, insects as well as mice and rats. Some researchers have suggested that cat domestication occurred alongside contact with mice and other vermin in the same area of the Middle East where agriculture first developed. *Scientific American* gives a date of around ten thousand years ago (Driscoll et al. 2009), but it was more likely eleven and a half thousand years ago or 9500 BCE as evidenced by the human/cat burial found on Cyprus. Serpell (2014, 86–87) comments:

Since its formation, the island of Cyprus has remained separated from mainland Asia Minor by a distance of some 60–80 km. As a result, it has no native cat species. Nevertheless, excavations on Cyprus dating from about 9,500 years before the current era (BCE) have unearthed the unmistakable remains of cats, one of which was buried in association with a person. The relatively large size of these animals suggests that they belonged to the subspecies *libyca*, and their presence on the island, living and dying in association with people, strongly implies that they were tamed and brought there in boats by the first human colonists. Assuming that Cyprus was not an isolated instance of cat taming, these discoveries indicate that the early Neolithic inhabitants of the Levant were already in the habit of capturing and taming wildcats, and taking them on ocean voyages at least as early as 10,000 years BCE. . . . Significantly, this date also closely corresponds to the date when the domestic cat lineage is believed to have separated from *libyca* origins based on genetic evidence.

As I have stated elsewhere:

The date of 10,000 BCE is interesting because 10,900 BCE is the date when parts of a comet apparently struck Canada and Northern Europe ushering in a mini-ice age called the Younger Dryas which lasted until around 9,600 BCE. It is after this catastrophic event that a "new" culture and cultural patterns emerge known as the Neolithic, which in many ways were a continuation of the patterns going on before 10,900 BCE, or what could be called the Proto-Neolithic. Some of the knowledge base of that prior time (10,900 BCE), including many of the cosmological features we see in the night sky (the zodiac), was already available as far back as 15,500 BCE (Sweatman 2019, 186–91). This catastrophic event would have pushed animals southward, and as water was tied up in glaciers, it would be easy to go from the Levant westward into Egypt and Libya. (Rush 2021a, 97)

But there are other possibilities for cat domestication. The now Libyan Desert was once a thriving grassland complete with lakes, marshes, cattle-herding humans, and lots of mice enjoying the same food as the cows. With the climate change beginning around 5600 BCE, the cattle herders moved southeast toward the Nile and what is "Upper Egypt" (because the Nile River flows north, Upper Egypt is in southern Egypt, while Lower Egypt is in the north, the Delta area). Humans cared for the cattle and were likely followed by cats (*Felis silvestris lybica* or *Felis chaus*) who were rewarded with a steady food supply: mice. Remember that cats have always seen us as a food supply, if not directly then indirectly through mice or a can of tuna.

The cat, as a mouser, was likely in Egypt more than seven thousand years ago, but its worth had to be appreciated in a practical sense and then, mythologically, its characteristics attached to gods and goddesses, both good and evil. At some point, either in the Levant or Egypt proper, the cat made some small alterations to its genetic code resulting in lower stress when relating to humans. It is common that when treated kindly, without threat, and with a regular food supply many animals (like squirrels, chipmunks, and birds) will acclimate to the presence of humans. Our ancestors were the ultimate anthropologists who participated in nature (being part of nature), but at the same time were able to stand back (apart) from nature, extract ideas for purposes of survival, and press them back in. And, as mentioned earlier, many qualities in nature we attach to ourselves—we desire power so we symbolically attach ourselves to lions, tigers, and other powerful animals. We saw ourselves in the behaviors and characteristics of these animals and perhaps more so in *Felis,* a predator that could be studied up close and personal without danger to life and limb—for the most part.

Quoting from Saunders:

Felines have had a profound effect on human sensibilities since the beginning of recorded time. The lion, leopard, tiger, jaguar, and puma have evoked a diversity of cultural responses across the world, and throughout history. In art, myth, ideology, and religious belief, many societies have employed feline icons as metaphors to express human qualities and symbolize human relations.

Any meaningful analysis of feline imagery in the Americas should acknowledge that it is part of a wider appraisal of human-animal as well as human-feline relationships. . . .

In considering the question "why the feline?" several points should be made. Significantly, apart from humans, felines are the most widespread and successful land-bound predators that evolution has produced. . . . In almost every region of the world that humans colonized, they came into competition with large felines—the most specialized of living carnivores . . . already present, and superbly adapted to their physical environment . . . selective processes that shaped human society may have been applicable to predators which were ecologically but not necessarily phylogenetically similar. (1998, 1)

The point is, humans and felines have been coadapting for millions of years, and the stress experienced on both sides is what eventually lead to our intense relationship with the domesticated cat.

3

Cat Behaviors and Physiology

All cats have different personalities and associated behaviors. However, like humans there are generalizations that can be made. Some cats are rather passive, some are uptight, on edge when awake, while others are in between. Others, again, are aggressive and assertive, while some stand back, out of the limelight. Domestic cats can be noisy or talkative, while others make little or no sounds at all besides purring. There are genetic issues connected to these behaviors, as animal breeders learned years ago when they picked out the gentler sheep, horses, and dogs.

POWER

Predatory cats, specifically the lion as in the Egyptian tradition, are symbolic of power. This, however, transfers to the domestic cat as a spiritual issue especially when it comes to guarding or protecting others. However, power can be used for evil purposes that are perhaps not spiritual in a general sense, although some religious groups might disagree. Killing in the name of a deity, as we find in monotheistic traditions, is considered a spiritual act with great rewards in heaven. Read the Old Testament and the orders of the deity, and of course Allah or il Leah, the Moon God of War, and the numerous war verses in the *Glorious Qur'an*; those verses and the actions of the true believers say it all for Islam—on a day-to-day basis, I might add. In Christianity, however, Jesus cannot be connected to war or killing in any way. Yes, there is the "sword" verse, but that is metaphorical of the division Jesus would create by suggesting that people be decent to one another, something world leaders put aside in favor of their own self-interests, as we can see with our modern medieval warlord, Vladimir Putin, sacking the city of Kiev.

Again, power and spirituality connected to the domestic cat emerges from their territorial imperative, their acute hearing, and their ability to see in low light conditions. Snakes are known to seek out dark secluded places, like temples, and thus cats added a measure of security.

NOISE

Cats are skittish, especially when it comes to novel objects and certainly unexpected noise; humans respond in the same manner: "Incoming!!!" These quick reactions have obvious survival value. Moreover, cats can hear sounds we cannot and can alert us when intruders enter their (and our) territory. As with power in general, the ability to sense danger and warn a temple priest would be considered spiritual behavior. "Thank the gods for cats!"

TALKING

"In the beginning was the word." These are sentiments carved into the Shabaka Stone dating to the twenty-fifth dynasty or 746–653 BCE, but they date to the Old Kingdom (circa 2649–2150 BCE). These sentiments are also found in the very beginning of the Gospel of St. John in the New Testament. Some cats when talked to, like my cat Spike, will talk back and actually continue a "conversation" for a minute or so. No other animal (with crows, ravens, and párrots as possible exceptions) will converse with the human animal to the same degree, at least in my experience. Being able to speak was conceived as magical and spiritual. The word *hieroglyphic* comes from the Greek *hieroglyphikos* meaning sacred carvings, and these carvings originate with the word. We think of these carvings and written script as art, but that is not the case. Such images were sacred, and, in many instances, never to be seen by human eyes once tombs were closed. As noted on the Shabaka Stone, the universe came into being through the word of Ptah (or Amun or Re, depending on which story you read during which time period) and thus words were sacred and caused things to happen; that would make cat talk, in its own way, spiritual and sacred.

CORRALLING

Another interesting behavior involves leading me somewhere. It would appear that at times Spike, Sid, or one of the gingers wants me to go to some place. To do this, they will walk in front of me, forcing me to go either right or left. This often happens when one of the cats wants me to go into the TV room. Once in the room the cat will usually go through the cat window and into the smaller of the two "catios" or come up onto my lap. Sid will also corral my wife Katie and lead her to the bedroom, where he will prompt her to brush his fur. As a longhair with a mane, he gets "dreadlocks" under his chin, and he needs to be brushed frequently. It is as if they either want something or simply want us close by and visible.

One of the gingers, usually Nate, will often lead me to something, perhaps a plastic bag he found, one of Katie's elastic hair ties, or another object he has dragged off a table. It is if he wants to lead me to a prize. I can imagine a cat corralling a temple priest in order to show him a dead cobra.

Another behavior, that is somewhat dangerous, is for Spike to walk back and forth in front of me when I am walking into the TV or living room. I'm not sure of the motive; perhaps it is a variation on corralling. Falling is not one of my favorite things, so I usually slow up and let Spike go further in front of me.

Corralling also signals interest in the one being corralled. We like to be liked, and cats do not make judgments as to how we look. They, like dogs, are very accepting animals, and to accept others, regardless of physical appearance or condition, is spiritual; it is unfortunate humans cannot be more like cats and dogs in this respect.

Several of our indoor cats, for want of better words, appear to "show off." We have several hemp-wrapped four-by-four posts in the living area that the cats love to climb. Two of the gingers, Nate and Ernie, will run about halfway up the pole and then look over a Katie or myself as we are walking by as if saying "See me!" With encouragement Nate will rapidly go to the top. Ernie, on the other hand, usually only goes half-way up, and even with encouragement jumps off midway. In his younger years, Spike would parade around the living area with a four-foot mop in his maw, making sure we saw him before he would struggle to get it through the doorway and into the kitchen, where he would drop in on the floor next to the stove. I always thought showing off was a human trait, but when you see how turkeys and other birds "show off" to get the attention of the female (sexual signaling) or to ward off a predator, this must be a behavior attached to the genome millions of years ago. Think about it: an animal showing off to a human. A temple priest would have perhaps recognized showing off as the behavior of a child and thus a connection to human agency.

MAKING BREAD OR PAWING

According to some cat researchers, making bread, or pawing, is instinctive and initially related to stimulating the flow of milk in the mother. When this carries over into adulthood the suggestion is it means "contentment" (Paoletta 2018). Some say it's a sign of love, a spiritual condition.

TERRITORIALITY

Cats are highly territorial, and this makes sense for any animal that needs a large enough territory to fulfill its caloric needs. Humans, for millions of years, had to rely on specific areas, and when we begin to see projectile points in human bone at archaeological sites, territoriality reveals its ugly head. There is a will to life and you have to eat to maintain life, and anything interfering with life will generate stress and conflict. Gang activity in big cities is a perfect example of this ancient need, for in the ghetto, in many cases, territory is all you have and it will be marked and defended. Humans mark territory with visual signs—this is called graffiti. But it is very important in that it informs of ownership and consequences. Individual taggers are actually doing the same thing, but in a more restricted manner. Their graffiti *is* the territory and signals "I was here."

Cats announce territory with urine and other scent markings, and it is the other scent marking from glands on the sides of their head and anus, in most cases, that signal ownership to the cat, but we interpret it as affection when a cat rubs its head or butt on us. And I don't think there is anything more spiritual than having affection for another. This is part of the bonding we have with cats, although it is misunderstood by the human agent. The cat is marking territory when he or she rubs its head against a leg or arm; when that tail is wrapped around your leg, your cat is actually rubbing secretions from anal glands located left and right of the anus proper. Most people can't detect this odor, but other cats (and dogs) can. We have seven highly domesticated cats that roam around most of the house, and they are continually rubbing themselves on Katie and myself. I think, in some cases, it is a means of covering the scent of one of the other cats. They walk across us, sit on us, and so on; we are part of their territory. This brings us to bonding.

BONDING

Humans are a small-group animal as are wolves. That is to say, for millions and millions of years our ancestors lived and died among only a small number of individuals. These numbers have been calculated by anthropologists to be between twenty-five and sixty individuals, forming relationships with other groups mainly for breeding purposes. As hunter-gatherers there are only so many calories in any given territory and this is often seasonal. Herd animals, like the Serengeti impala or waterbuck, travel in much larger groups, which is possible because the Serengeti plains provide lots of grass for these herbivores.

On the other side, cats are not small-group animals. Yes, lions hang out in a pride, but the domesticated cat is more closely related to leopard-like cats, that is the puma, lynx, or bobcat, which are loners. My experience with both feral and domesticated cats is they will closely bond with another cat. Currently we have a new, young feral on the property, and it has already bonded with Sandy (the mother of the gingers in our home) and Rocky, a domesticated cat who prefers being outside.

Cats from the same litter form close bonds with those born close to them (birth order) or who feed next to one another on the queen's nipples. Our cats tend to look after one another especially when they are sick or injured. They even become more sensitive to Katie and me when we are ill. This is especially the case for the females. Our female Maine Coon (Daisey) alerts us when one of the other cats is closed up in a closet (a common occurrence) or room or when one of the other cats is ill. She will sometimes curl up next to a sick cat, apparently keeping the other warm. There are even stories of female cats acting as surrogate mothers to squirrels and rabbits (Mullarkey 2021). Currently, one of our gingers, Nate, is ill, perhaps from something he ate. While getting him ready for the trip to the vet hospital, we brought out the cat carrier and right away we could see the anxiety in another ginger, Sherbet (Sherb for short), his brother. Anyway, they know that when the cat carrier comes out, it means a trip to that strange place and those strange people, and something isn't right. The night before it was Sherb who curled up next to Nate to keep him warm, and as I write this Sherb is sleeping in Nate's spot on the bed, something I've never see him do. Sleeping spots are "sacred" territory, at least for our cats. How do we explain this behavior for a loner species and not a small-group animal? Perhaps cats are becoming small-group animals. This type of behavior has been seen in other species, wolves and elephants, for example, although they are a highly social animal and the behavior is not surprising. Katie and I have seen this "caring" behavior in cats many, many times over the past thirty-five years.

Some years ago, we had a cat we named Scruffy, a beautiful white and beige longhair. He was possibly hit by a car and had a broken leg, but somehow he managed to get back to the house. We noticed that one of the other older cats living with us at the time, a male who usually stayed close by the house, disappeared for long periods of time during a three-day period, and he apparently helped Scruffy get back home. We took Scruffy to the vet, they set his leg (it was a lengthy surgery), and he had to stay in a cage for about a month before we could safely allow him access to the outside. He was never the same; he became grumpy and picked on the other outside cats, so we changed his name from Scruffy to Scrumpy.

Cats will form very strong bonds with singular humans although they will mark others in a family as territory. Like with humans, when you give positives you usually get positives in return. I am reminded of Aesop's tale of "Androcles and the Lion."

A slave by the name of Androcles escaped from his master and fled into a forested area not knowing what fate was to befall him. Wandering alone he could hear moans and groans coming from some thick underbrush. Cautiously he pulled back a branch or two and, jumping back, he came face to face with a lion—the biggest lion he had ever seen! He turned to flee, but the lion continued to moan and groan and was not the least bit interested in Androcles. So out of curiosity he went back to the lion, and as he did the lion put out his paw, and Androcles could see it was bloody and swollen. Very cautiously he approached, being careful not to make direct eye contact. He could see the problem: a thorn was deeply embedded in the lion's paw. Cautiously, he removed the thorn, at which point the lion let out a weak roar, but Androcles, containing his fear the best he could, removed an unsoiled piece of his waist garment and bound the paw to stop the bleeding, at which point the lion bent over and licked the hand of Androcles like a dog. He then helped the lion to a nearby cave, where Androcles could change his underwear and bring the poor lion meat each day, as he was not able to hunt by himself.

But shortly afterward both Androcles and the lion were captured, and the slave was sentenced to be thrown to the lions, which had been kept without food for several days.

The emperor and all his court came to see the spectacle, and Androcles was led out into the middle of the arena. Soon a lion was let loose from his den and rushed bounding and roaring toward his victim. But as soon as he came near to Androcles he recognized his friend, fawned upon him, and licked his hands like a friendly dog.

The emperor, surprised at this, summoned Androcles to him, who told him the whole story. Whereupon the slave was pardoned and freed and the lion let loose in his native forest.

There is a 1953 movie, *Androcles and the Lion,* based on the 1912 George Bernard Shaw play of the same name. A similar story is told of St. Jerome (Voragine 1993, Vol. II, 211–16), (who, by the way, was never able to rid himself of his erotic desires—this is why he spent most of his time isolated in the desert):

Jerome was a noted scholar and became a cardinal at age 39. Not interested in papal politics, he lived as a hermit for four years, his only companions being scorpions and wild animals. Eventually he went to Bethlehem, living at the place of the Nativity, working on his translation of the Bible.

One day while Jerome was praying at the monastery, a lion wandered by striking fear into the attending monks. Jerome, on the other hand, stayed calm and removed the thorn from the lion's paw and properly washed and bandaged the wound. From that moment on the lion remained among the monks, guarding the donkey when it carried wood in from the fields.

One day, however, thieves entered the grounds and stole the donkey and the monks assumed that the lion ate it. As punishment the lion was assigned the donkey's task of carrying wood. The lion patiently put up with the burden but also continued to look for the donkey. One day the thieves, who were camel merchants, returned and there was the donkey. With a terrifying roar the lion scattered the merchants who abandoned their camels and the donkey, which the lion led back to the monastery. Jerome realized what had happened, the merchants reappeared asking forgiveness, and Jerome offered forgiveness and he, the lion, and the donkey lived happily ever after.*

How can we explain this behavior, the metaphor of a cat caring for another animal it would usually eat without hesitation? It is difficult to generalize across the board, but I think it is entirely possible that our ancestors serving as the cat's main source of food conditioned them to alter their DNA in such a way as to develop a dependency *on* our ancestors. Keep in mind that a predator that lives almost exclusively on animal flesh experiences stress day after day, for without the necessary protein, it will die. A domesticated cat can only go a few days without food. So, like humans who have a deep, probably genetic urge to explore, the cat may have a deep yearning or caring for us, not

---

*Paraphrased from McIntosh 2020.

necessarily out of love, but as a food source, reinforced by the fact that we consistently feed them. In this sense, we are still their food. The difference is now they don't have to work so hard for their calories. This caring becomes generalized and transfers onto the humans with whom they bond. When your cat looks longingly at you, what does it actually see in a primordial sense? Right—meat. This is not much different from a man longingly looking at a woman or a woman looking longingly at a man. Those primal urges are ever present. Now you know part of the meaning of the Tree of Knowledge in the Garden of Eden. You are aware of your lusty animal nature, which has to be tamed if what we call culture, with all its morality and rules, *constructed out of social necessity,* can emerge. Knowledge forces rules and regulations into existence if we are to survive. Most of us, although belonging to small groups, are surrounded by strangers, that is, others and their small groups, and bits of most religions at least inform that if we can't get along, we will perish. But the story goes deeper and calls for our need to relate to nature in a positive manner—and this includes the wild animals.

In any case, we speak of love as part of the emotional bond, and that is precisely what love is. It is the capacity to care for others, practiced by many animals, cats included. Love is nothing special; it is not a magical part of our positive emotions, contrary to what some researchers say for example, Desmond Morris in his video presentation *The Biology of Love.* Sex urges are genetically designed for immortality. Love is a different issue and basically equals positives, as perceived by the receiver. Feral cats bond to me, not out of any special love, but because I bring them food, which they obviously see as positive, a very important positive. Humans need food as well and see a full belly as positive, but as a small-group animal, humans have a biological need to receive positives from another or the group—"man does not live by bread alone"—humans need to know they belong and are accepted. Cats do not need this to the same extent as humans, although there are exceptions, but your dog as a small-group animal does. Cats seem to live in two worlds, which can translate into the upper (domestic) and lower (wild, dangerous) worlds and are confined to neither.

The territorial behavior of cats was, at least in part, misunderstood by our ancestors and even today. The cat is staking out a territory, and if there is plenty of food the cat will continue to mark you as part of its territory. Remember that cats likely do not realize where their food miraculously comes from. To the cat it comes from living in a territory that includes you as the food.

There is an old trick regarding bonding. For newborn cats, if you breathe onto the face of the cat, it will bond to you more quickly. Smell is very important to cats. This may be one of the techniques used ten or eleven thousand years ago in the Middle East when we first began domesticating cows, sheep, goats, and cats—the breath of life.

There is another way to make friends with a cat and that is through eye winks. It is because of the eyes, among other traits, that cats are seen as mystical. One of our gingers, Nate, lifts his head up and squints at me. I return the favor and slowly blink both eyes. Usually cats avoid direct eye contact, especially with other cats. Holding eye contact is a threat gesture; instead they glance and look away. Cats seem to respond positively to slow eye blinks by not averting eye contact but instead maintaining it, especially if the human element continues with slow eye blinks (Rush 2021a, 147–48).

Human and cat bonding, as mentioned, can be very intense, which may signal, as mentioned, a genetic change in cats over the millennia. One of my cats, Spike, a Maine Coon, is so attached to me he has to know where I am at all times, often roaming the house calling out my name—the best he can. This devotion cats can have for specific individuals was noticed by priests and others. Those who do a lot for others, for example, cook for the elderly, look out for friends and relatives, are giving positives, especially when giving food as this says the person is included. There is nothing worse than feeling excluded, as exclusion equals symbolic death. This giving of self without an expectation of return is considered spiritual, a behavior considered worthy of saint-hood in the Catholic tradition.

INDEPENDENCE

An important feature of the cat is independence. This comes across as indifference. All our inside cats know their names and respond to them—when they want to, when they will get something, like time with the laser dot or a special treat of whitefish or tuna paté.*

As a small-group animal, independence can only go so far; our overall survival depends on belonging to a group, family, work, or peer group, and so on. And we see what happens when individuals get dis-connected from groups: the loneliness, sadness, and oftentimes bitter-ness; this bitterness can be turned inward resulting in depression, drug abuse (or worse) or turned outward in terms of violence. This is very common in urban settings, where a single person is no one. You have to belong to a group to be someone, to have a social identity. Further, once you are part of an urban setting you become a slave to that environ-ment, for it is in that space you obtain food, housing, and police protec-tion. Only a very few with specific skills and money can pack their bags, move to the hills, and make a living without need of a shopping mall or a country store. Hermits come close to this, but even hermits are not totally self-sufficient. Many have chosen to "live off the grid" and move to isolated locations. Although they live off the grid individuals will often form coalitions where vegetables are traded for meat or firewood is traded for ammunition, and so on. Actually, one can live off the grid and never leave town; barter groups have been common in the United

---

*Most of the food available to the cats is high-quality kibble, which means they need more water than a cat in the wild living off mice. For eating habits of the domesticated cat see Rush 2021a.

States for many years. Street people, for the most part, live off the grid and obtain food and clothes through barter, panhandling, or theft. Dogs and cats often fill the void of human companionship especially for the elderly and the down and out in our culture.

Dependence and being depended upon has its limits, and at times we all crave space. "I want to be alone. I just want to be alone!" as Greta Garbo said in the 1932 movie classic *Grand Hotel*. Cat independence, in my opinion, arises from the fact that cats are not a small-group animal like dogs, wolves, and humans. They are flexible opportunists and can get along in groups, assuming plenty of food and territory, but they appear to be programmed, as well, to go it alone. This independence would have been noticed by our ancestors as otherworldly, a suggestion that they take direction from the gods, and not solely humans.

REJECTION

Sam Westreich (2020) suggests that cats don't hold grudges, but I'm not so sure. I guess it depends on what the "grudge" is. Cats certainly remember when they are treated badly (just as humans do) and by whom, and this might qualify as holding a grudge. But what about rejection—do cats show rejection toward their owners? In my opinion, they do. Cats bond to specific individual. The individual becomes territory, and when other cats come onto that territory (sit in one's lap), this is psychologically troubling to the cat, as would be the case living in the wild during an encounter with another cat in one's territory; this can lead to violence. Jealousy likewise seems to be part of the cat bonding process, as it is with humans. We often jealously guard relationships; we don't like sharing our close friends. Spike, a Maine Coon who is closely bonded to me, will jump up onto my chair, notice a cat sitting on me, and then turn his back to me. This "rejecting behavior," fortunately, does not seem to last long and usually stops with some low voice tones or light touching. Is rejection spiritual? I'm not sure it would qualify, but it is a human behavior, and any behavior that appears human might be labeled spiritual, especially by a "spiritual" person like a priest.

STARING INTO SPACE

Cats, as discussed, have finely tuned sensory systems. They can detect slight, rapid movements, and they can hear sounds way above what is normal for humans. Several of our indoor cats watch TV, although determining whether or not they are following the story line is problematic at best. But they certainly pay attention when a cat, during a commercial for example, "talks." At times, however, cats just stare into space, perhaps daydreaming, but it appears their minds just shut off. However this behavior might be seen as a form of meditation, a spiritual behavior, to clear one's mind and merge with the universe. I will come back to this behavior when I discuss dreaming in chapter 7.

STRETCHING

Ancient Egyptian hieroglyphs often display humans, baboons (Thoth, who is likewise depicted as an Ibis, representing knowledge or civilized, while his animal persona is a baboon), and lions stretched out on the ground in reverence to Re the sun god or Pharaoh, the Sun God incarnate. With what appears to be a greeting ritual, cats will often do a "stretch-em-out" accompanied by a yawn, and this would have been seen as reverence of the cat for a priest or anyone with whom the cat had bonded—a spiritual act. We are told that the stretching is a form of exercise but could also mean they are relaxed and comfortable (National Center for Families Learning, "Why Do Cats Stretch"). However, in my opinion, it goes deeper than that. We greet each other verbally; their nonverbal gestures and the frequency that cats engage in this stretched-out behavior suggest it is likewise a greeting gesture. It is unlikely simply a means of exercising. Of all the behaviors attributed to cats, stretching out in front of a priest, for example, would appear to be one of the most obvious of spiritual acts, that is, reverence toward human agency.

HIDDEN PLACES AND ESCAPE ROUTES

Cats have an uncanny ability to find dark, out-of-the way places to hide or sleep. As one is vulnerable when asleep, especially if in a CATatonic state, dark, out-of-the way places offer sanctuary.

Sandy, our outside queen ginger, gave birth to eight kittens, but one was stillborn. The other seven were cute from the beginning. Sandy would allow us to come into the cage and clean up litter and spilled water or kibble but would not accept touching. She was, however, a devoted mother.

As the days went on, the kittens opened their eyes, and it became apparent that three of the seven had the ocular herpes virus and Katie and I would put drops in their eyes twice a day. Four weeks went by and they started to eat some of the kitten kibble. By this time Sandy was getting anxious, so after the about the sixth week we opened the cage and off she went. She came back in twice with her new friend, Rocky, and the kittens came up to her wanting to get fed, but she did not seem to pay much attention to them.

After the morning feeding, at age six weeks, we would let the kittens into my study, which adjoins the birthing area. The first two or three days it was a matter of sniffing around coming up on the bed, and so on, but one day that changed.

One morning Katie let them into my study and left the room for a moment, and when she came back she could only locate five of the seven. Panicking, she looked under the bed, in their cage, under my desk, all possible places but to no avail. She came back out in the living room and suggested they must have gotten outside, so I came into the study to investigate. This time there were only three of the seven, playing on the bed. It would be impossible for them to go outside, and they weren't in obvious places in the room, so where could they have gone? Just to be sure Katie and I went outside, checking the front and back—nothing. Coming back into the study, no kittens were visible; they were not in the room! Could this be a case of alien cat abduction? Then we heard a little squeak coming from the dresser in the corner. I opened the top drawers, nothing. I opened the middle drawer, and all curled up together, among my socks, were seven sleeping kittens. I am not exactly sure how they got into the drawer—from underneath, I suppose, as there is a crawl space and entrance through the back of the drawer. From then on, that drawer was the place to be and they all ended up there for several hours each morning, at least for three or four weeks, at which point they were too big. It would seem that cats will instinctively hunt for out-of-the-way places that are basically enclosed from all sides, as such spaces are easy to defend. But cats also look for escape routes (Rush 2021a, 167–68).

This need for dark, secluded places would relate to the Underworld, and although the Underworld was a place of judgment, with the right rituals one can pass through the gates, have one's heart weighed against the feather (Ma'at), and then be escorted by Horus to Osiris and the Field of Reeds. These characteristics connect them to the Underworld, and, along with the protection of Re (in the form of a cat) against the evil Apepi/Apophis, qualify as spiritual.

MATING BEHAVIOR AND FERTILITY

I am not sure that many would place mating behavior into the category of spiritual (tantric sex and sex in ritual/religious settings are exceptions). We can romanticize human mating in books and movies, but for the most part this is portrayed as carnal. The female feline has behaviors that could most certainly be seen as analogous to human wants and needs, that is, the passion or genetically programmed "push" for sex and thus immortality. An interesting play on uncontrolled impulses can be found in medieval Christian art where the female cat in heat is noted, with butt in the air; this image has been translated as either an insult to some important member of the court or to draw attention to perhaps immoral behavior (Nastyuk 2019).

Thus the image of a cat with its butt in the air was a statement about morality. This would have been an extension of the "agent of the devil" mantra cooked up by the Catholic Church in order to purge any influence from competitive religious systems and, in my opinion, the cat symbol from ancient Egypt.

The persecution of cats by the Catholic Church during the Middle Ages, that is, stating that cats were succubi or agents of the devil, may have its origins in ancient Egypt and their animal cults. Cats were often purchased by pilgrims, sacrificed, mummified, and used as vehicles for communicating with the deities to ask favors or perhaps as oracles to tell the future. The animal cults in Egypt were most active when the ancient Egyptian ways were on the wane and Christianity was on the rise.

This idea of messengers of the gods, considered evil by the Catholic Church because this belief represented competition for the minds and souls of their subjects, is perhaps the origin of the belief in cats being agents of the devil. The devil represented the major symbol of evil in Christianity, a symbol that embodied a reference to *all* deities connected to competitive systems. The horned devil is often connected to the Greek god Pan who is half man and half goat and represents the basic instincts, such as lust. But there are other connections to, for example, the Green Man in some of the current Wiccan (Celtic) traditions, who represents renewal. The Green Man likewise reflects Cernunnos, an antlered fertility god in the original Celtic tradition (circa 500 BCE) who sits in a lotus position surrounded by animals and henbane, a mind-altering herb alleged to be one of the ingredients in the original Witches Brew (Rush 2021a, 171–72).

Fertility, on the other side, is an absolute necessity, referring to crops or food and of course live births. Cats, as noted, reproduce quickly, and numbers count. The domesticated cat can have, as mentioned, up to seven or eight in a litter and can produce up to five litters per year! Moreover, in the Egyptian urban environment many of those in a litter will survive; this is not necessarily the case in the wild where the domestic cat (as well as *Felis chaus* and *Felis silvestris lybica*) are prey animals to larger predators. Min, one of the original fertility gods in ancient Egypt, and Tammuz in Mesopotamia are conceptualized as male and, like the Egyptian pharaoh, responsible for crop fertility. The pharaoh spent most of his waking moments in ritual process to make sure the gods were pleased and continued to provide crops. Tammuz is depicted on an alabaster relief from Ashur, dated to circa 1500 BCE, flanked by two lions. Tammuz's wife is Inanna, and she is likewise connected to lions, symbols of power and fertility (Britannica, "Tamuz"). Fertility, then, would be seen as necessary and certainly spiritual in ancient Egypt, as demonstrated in the form of the cat, Bastet.

GROOMING BEHAVIOR

There are three basic things cats are good at: eating, sleeping, and grooming. Cats are very clean animals if given a clean environment. I have noticed with our domesticated house cats there are two behaviors that commence once grooming is completed: the cat will fall asleep or it will walk its conditioned territory, noting new smells and applying scent to surfaces that had been wiped down or dusted or new objects encountered, including clothing. This would have been noticed by the temple priest who likewise must perform ablution or a ritual cleansing before servicing the gods (making offerings, etc.). As an example, Spike, the Maine Coon, will sit beside me in the morning when Katie and I have coffee, groom for perhaps five or ten minutes, and then jump down from the chair, make his way out of the living room, and "make bread" on the cardboard scratching pad, after which he tags, with his forehead, the front door. He then makes his way down the hall, visits the bathroom, continues down the hall into the TV room, and then out to the catio on the east side of the house. He will remain there for perhaps several minutes (sometimes longer) and then retrace his steps, enter the first kitchen, and then go into the auxiliary kitchen and up onto a windowsill that looks out onto the west side of the property. Here he can get a good look at cats, birds, and squirrels in the back yard. He then jumps down and exits the auxiliary kitchen via a cat door which enters into the larger catio on the northwest side of the property. Spike has a special place in the larger catio, a pad near the ceiling that allows full view of the back yard. This is an everyday journey from room to room, visiting those places of comfort, places of familiarity—his territory—examining and tagging the new and the old.

Imagine, if you will, a temple in Egypt, complete with numerous rooms furnished with hieroglyphs and statues of gods, and temple cats first grooming (ablutions) and then visiting room after room tagging with headbutts, and perhaps stretching out when meeting a priest, wrapping its tail around the priest's leg, and leaving a scent marking. This behavior could appear to be similar to the priest's behavior when servicing the gods; priests have their territories as well.

Reviewing, then, power could be seen as the cat's most prominent characteristic. This is evidenced by shamans wearing jaguar skins, the leopard-skinned chief in numerous cultures, the lion-headed gods and goddesses, the shape-shifting abilities, the ability to cause chaos and other miseries, and so on. The characteristic of power would translate into the category of spiritual. Our ancient ancestors didn't necessarily see themselves as powerful, having, as they did, to borrow the characteristic from animals they obviously saw as powerful, the predators—in this case, cats. Power is bestowed by the gods, thus the power of cats must come from otherworldly sources and is therefore spiritual.

Talking would be another spiritual behavior not encountered in cows, bulls, chickens, or any of the other animals available to our ancestors. Although cats are by no means the only animal that vocalizes with humans, they do seem to try harder as a means of being like us. Speaking, as noted, brings the universe into existence ("In the beginning was the word"), thus the cat's vocalization and spirituality.

Bonding is a very important issue, for although bonding between humans is natural and expected as we are a small-group animal, humans make judgments regarding size, skin color, or whether male or female—cats do not.

Stretching, especially when encountering a priest or a person to which the cat has bonded, would have been seen as praise or reverence, just as baboons and others, as displayed in the hieroglyphs, prostrate themselves on the ground in front of Re or Pharaoh, the Sun God and the Son of the Sun. The Son of the Sun or the Son of God theme is a very old one.

The nature of the cat to seek out dark, secluded places and their glowing eyes would connect the cat to the Underworld. This would certainly be reinforced by the morphing of Re into a cat in the Underworld as protection against dark forces, for example, Apepi or Apophis. As protectors or guardians in the Underworld, and as protectors against snakes and scorpions in the Upper World, cats would certainly qualify as spiritual, but unlike us, they have a "foot" in each world.

Fertility is an absolute concern for the opposite of fertility is infertility and death. Thus, in the same way as some Gallic cultures see the rabbit or hare (*Ostara* or *Eastre*—Easter) as a symbol of fertility and spring time, the Egyptians saw the cat.

Spiritual cleansing before administering to the gods was an absolute necessity for priests in ancient Egypt and even today. In the writing of Herodotus (2017) we encounter numerous behaviors Egyptians used that were designed to keep the body clean. This was a necessity, for with close living in that climate, lice and other pests were a problem; body odor was considered offensive as well. Head lice were addressed with cosmetics and by shaving off all body and head hair. Women also shaved, and this is one reason for the wigs, especially worn at parties. They also used tree resin as a breath mint.

From what has been presented thus far, I feel confident in saying that the cat was not worshipped in ancient Egypt or anywhere else. In

Egypt, cat fat was used to keep away mice as well as in medicinal recipes (see below). The Irish, at least in their mythology, applied cat skins to their war helmets. In Hinduism, Jainism, and Buddhism, cats freely walk the temples and are taken care of, although there are monster cats as well. Realize, however, that taking a life (outside of vegetable life) can attract bad karma as all lifeforms are as one. Cows walk the streets, monkeys (potentially very dangerous, by the way) inhabit the temples, as do rats. Anywhere you have free meat, cats are likely diners, not gods to be worshipped. Besides, all was Buddha consciousness—the trees, rocks, birds and cats; all were god.

Going back to ancient Egypt, I want to repeat that the cat was demonized in medieval Europe, and, in part, this was likely connected to the animal cults at Saqqara, Sharuna, Tanis, Tel Basta, Thebes, and other locations. Such cults became more active as the ancient Egyptian civilization started fading away and the religious traditions started being replaced by Christianity. At these locations numerous types of animals, and, for the moment, cats, were sacrificed, mummified, and available for pilgrims wishing to send messages to the gods (Ikram 2015).

But the cat has likely always had demonic qualities, for it ate our ancestors on a daily basis. The positive aspects of cats became apparent when we learned how to process carcasses left by large predators and then more so when we intimately included cats in our lives perhaps twelve thousand years ago. We had to adapt to cats, and they had to adapt to us, and from this we can see the cat in ourselves. In my opinion the more recent demonizing of cats, beginning with the witch hunts in Europe, was not motivated by evil characteristics embedded in the cat, but instead stems from political and economic issues invented by the Catholic Church; the evil was embedded in the Church. Cave art of twenty to thirty thousand years ago does not suggest in any manner a demon cat even in terms of the lion, a powerful animal, that occasionally ate the cave artists. Keep in mind that lions like to live in shelters and caves, as did the bear, and an unsuspecting artist those many years ago was no match for a lion in that environment.

4

Animal Worship

Very few animals were worshipped in the ancient world. One of the problems is how we define worship; few authors make the distinction between worship, spiritual, holy, and so on, so some writers imagine that a god with a lion's head (e.g., Sekhmet) means worship of the lion rather than the god with characteristics of the lion. This is the confusion of a symbol with its reference.

FEW AND FAR BETWEEN

In ancient Egypt there were two animals that possibly qualify as "worshipped," the Apis bull and perhaps the crocodile Sobek. The Apis bull was connected to Re the sun god; Re's daughter is Hathor, the goddess with the horns of a cow as her determinative. The Apis bull had to be black with a white diamond shape on its forehead, the shape of a hawk's wing on its back, and so on. The bull would perhaps have a lifespan of twenty-five years, die, and then was mummified, placed in a sarcophagus (which means "flesh eater"), and entombed, for example at Saqqara (Ikram 2014). What I find interesting is we have instructions for mummifying a bull but not for mummifying a human. Some Egyptologists have suggested this is because mummification occurred on a daily basis and there would be no need to write down the instructions, and this may be true. However, as this procedure was highly ritualized it was perhaps proprietary and thus kept secret. Bull mummification, however, was rare, perhaps once every twenty or twenty-five years. But I think there could be another reason. Mummifying bodies was not done by the medical professionals and was not considered, in any way, a noble profession. In our own time we don't write biographies on mortuary workers (an unclean profession in some cultures) and we can presume the same for ancient Egypt. In fact, in our own time, morticians are often characterized as spooky and ghoulish.

The determinative for Sobek is the crocodile. It emerges from the shadowy depths of the Nile, the primeval waters or Nun, like a bump in the water, the Ben-Ben stone, the first land that emerged at the beginning of time in the Egyptian myths. Crocodiles, however, are very dangerous and likely ate many Egyptians. Sobek was also a healing and fertility god and protector and was likely worshipped in a similar way as devil worshippers worship the devil. That is to say, the good god will not hurt you—in the story of Job, for example, God's adversary does the dirty work, not God himself. God literally gives the adversary permission to torture and torment Job (does that seem demonic to you?). So, the rationale is, if the good god won't hurt you, then pay tribute to the one who will. You pay homage to Sobek so he will not harm you.

The claim by Davisson (2021, 14) that the cat was worshipped in Japan, a country fascinated with cats, is premature. Yes, shrines were set up referencing cats, but they were not worshipped like gods. Cats originally brought into Japan were very costly, and only the rich could afford them. Certainly, they were cuddled and pampered, but not worshipped. As time went on cats proliferated and eventually escaped the rich and famous, ending up in peasant villages. On their own and needing food they entered homes and barns, marking territories and being a general nuisance, but they were still considered pets by many. It is at this point that the cat was painted with various shades of evil. Japanese *kaibyō*, for example, were considered shape-shifters and vampires, often becoming symbols of evil after a certain age, in some renditions age seven. Any shrines to cats in Japan represent symbols of luck (the cat *yōkai* called *maneki-neko* in Japan and *zhāocái māo* in China), or a hedge against being visited by shape-shifting and vampire cats—they were not worshipped. Most of these stories are connected to Shintoism; the Buddhists in Japan, however, were rather cold toward cats. Yes, they may have kept the mouse population down thus protecting their manuscripts, but outside of that, the cat probably marked its territory, stole some of their food, didn't mourn with the passing of the Buddha, and so on. Most people think that *all* Buddhists see all life as sacred, but there appear to be different levels of sacredness.

WHAT IS A GOD

The term "god" has many dimensions. In monotheistic traditions the deity is all powerful and creates the universe as we experience it in the field of time. In a dualistic world, however, the monotheistic deity has to have a counterpart with perhaps equal power to unravel the creation and move toward nothingness; life can only exist alongside death. And so, there is always a tug-of-war, so to speak. In Judaism (Yahweh), Christianity (God the Father, *who is not Jesus*), and Islam (il-Liah or Allah), the deity is jealous and demands absolute worship forcing believers into a form of celestial slavery. Enki, in Sumerian myth, created humans to be slaves to the gods. Considered in those terms, many of the gods are actually demons, unless, of course, you don't mind being enslaved or if you see slavery as normal as it was in Egypt and many areas of the world for thousands of years (and still is, the sex trade being just one example). Antislavery is actually a fairly new concept.

In ancient Egypt there was a term, *neteru,* that could mean *the* god or the *gods,* indicating that monotheism was not a new idea, but for the Egyptians as well as the Sumerians, Mayans, and so on, polytheists all, one needed to explain natural phenomenon, and that required characteristics of the gods to emerge in order to organize, describe, and, in their own way, explain the world around them. For the Egyptians and most cultures, there is good and evil; there is power, for example, that can be beneficial and power that is destructive. Sekhmet can be a destroyer (the raging heat of the desert) but can also act on behalf of humans by destroying one's enemies.

The monotheists see their deity as all powerful and in control of all the forces of nature and life and death; monotheists see their traditions as being superior or more highly advanced than polytheistic traditions. In monotheistic traditions you, the true believer, can never be god, any more than you can be king or pharaoh; monotheistic traditions are traditions of worship, of supplication, and they divide people—you are either inside the group or outside. This division is very clear in Middle East politics. For polytheists, on the other side, the gods represent descriptions of forces of nature which the individual can *identify with and become.*

Gods, then, are forces, and thus they are described in terms of what is experienced *in* nature, which is often times dualistic. The scorpion is the *determinative* for the goddess Serquet who wears a scorpion on her head. Serquet is not the scorpion; this, again, is the confusion of a symbol with its reference. The ancient Egyptians reasoned that whatever could kill you could also cure you (the basis of homeopathic medicine), thus Serquet holds an ankh (a symbol of life in this context) and a *was-scepter,* likely symbolic of Seth, the evil brother of Osiris, but also symbolic of power. Sekhmet is the other side of Hathor, just as you have your aggressive side.

But gods can also be the instrument of creation when new traditions or new religions emerge. For example, the Babylonian god Marduk dismembers Tiamat after the goddess loses a battle with Marduk.

Marduk now pauses, gazing upon the dead body and considering the foul thing to devise an ingenious plan. Whereafter, he split her in two halves like a shellfish. He set one above, as a heavenly roof fixed with a crossbar, and assigned guards to watch her waters that she should not escape. He next traversed the heavens, surveyed its quarters, and, over against the Apsu (salt water) of his father Ea, measured the magnitude of the Deep. He then established upon this a great abode, the Earth, as a canopy above the Apsu. He assigned Anu, Enlil, and Ea to their various residences (namely, Heaven, Earth, and the Abyss), and the first part of his enterprise therewith had been accomplished (Campbell 1991, 83).

This is the dismembering of a former tradition but using the former as a base for constructing the new narrative. In the death rituals of ancient Egypt, the identity of each part of the deceased was that of a god. For example, "My eyes are the eyes of Thoth" is reminiscent of this in that the goal is rebirth, the new coming out of the old. There is a magical spell on the magical-medical Metternich Stela belonging to the reign of Nectanebo II, Thirtieth Dynasty, 360–343 BCE, carved into which is "Spells for Healing a Cat" (Allen 2005, 53–54):

Spell for enchanting a cat: O Sun, come for your daughter, for a scorpion has bitten her on the path alone! Her cry reaches above and is heard on your path. Poison has entered her body and pervaded her flesh. It has given its mouth to her. Look, the poison is in her body. So come with your control, with your wrath, with your redness! Look, it is hidden before you, having entered in every limb of this cat I'm treating.

Don't fear, don't fear, my effective daughter! Here I am around you. I am the one who feels for you the poison that is in any limb of this cat.

You cat, your head is the head of the Sun, the Two Lands' lord, who strikes disaffected subjects, fear of whom is in all lands and all the living forever. You cat, your eyes are the eye of the Effective Eye's owner, who illuminates the Two Lands with his eye, who illuminates the face in darkness's path. You cat, your nose is the nose of twice-great Thoth, lord of Hermopolis, chief of the Two Lands of the Sun, who gives air to the nose of every man. You cat, your ears are the ears of the Lord to the Limit, who hears the voice of every man when they call, who judges in the whole land. You cat, your mouth is the mouth of Atum, lord of life, the Unity: as he has given unity, he has saved you from every poison. You cat . . .

The spell goes on and on, associating different gods and goddesses with the cat's body parts. Two points: first, for a pharaoh—Nectanebo in this case (or which elite commissioned the carving of this stela)— to devote this to a cat suggests the importance of the cat at least at this point in history. The importance of the cat was such that "[w]hen a beloved cat died in ancient Egypt, its owners would shave their eyebrows as a sign of mourning" (Kennedy 2022, 25). And second, this is a clear statement that the cat, like all other worldly things, is subject to the slings and arrows of nature, and was not, in itself, worshipped as a god. Moreover, the spell indicates that scorpion stings must have been a common occurrence with cats, helping to reinforce their use as guardians and protectors.

HINDUISM, JAINISM, AND BUDDHISM

Let's consider Hinduism, Jainism, and Buddhism. The claim is that, in some cases, the cat was worshipped in these three related traditions. The problem here is that in these traditions *all* living things *are* god. This is the meaning behind hands folded together and the invocation *namaste.* This gesture represents recognition of the god *within,* not to be confused with any specific god. So in these traditions the cat is god *but so is everything.* Moreover, lifeforms are sacred, at least in their metaphysics; for example temple monkeys, rats, mice, cats, and so on. In the temples, for example, cats were welcome to help deal with mice, animals that will eat most anything including manuscripts produced from parchment but also leaves and other organic materials. But the mouse would be sacred as well. So you keep cats around to eat the mice. Are mice, then, less sacred than the cat?

USES OF THE CAT IN ANCIENT EGYPT

To further show that cats were not worshipped in ancient Egypt, let's consider how the cat was used. Cats were used in two general ways, that is, symbolically or spiritually and physically. Perhaps the most spiritual use of the cat was to send messages to the Otherworld, and, although our ancient ancestors did not sacrifice and mummify bears, they were used in a similar manner. The theory is our ancient ancestors used to go down into caves during the winter months, asking the hibernating bear to take messages to the other side, that is, for animals to come back for another meal (of course they are the meal). The ancient Egyptians did the same by first sacrificing the cat; the cat would then take the message to the spiritual world. The cat, then, was a shaman in a sense, but not quite the animal master as was the bear and the human shaman that followed. They did, however, communicate with the gods for favors, advice, and for a glimpse of the future. This communication also took place with relatives and the recently deceased, for it would be those judged by Osiris and now existing in the west, in the Field of Reeds, who would be in the best position to intercede on their behalf. This can be seen as a sort of psychotherapy; through the rites and ritual performed with the use of cats, one is taking action, and doing something is, in many cases, better than doing nothing at all.

Cats were also used to protect the grain in silos attached to palaces and temples; the cats were most valuable in this respect as Egypt was known as the "bread basket" of the Middle East. But cats were used in other ways, in ways one might consider spiritual in the sense of guarding against or repelling danger. For example, cat fat was smeared on areas to repel mice. As Germond (2001, 77) comments: "Cats also made a contribution to the spheres of magic and medicine, their fat, fur and feces being used in a number of preparations of somewhat doubtful efficacy. A medical papyrus specifies ' . . . to stop mice from coming near, smear everything with cat fat,' and the same ingredient appears in ointments for soothing burns, alleviating stiffness of the joints and preventing grey hair."

Reeves (1992, 12) comments further: "Sir William Flinders Petrie, the British Egyptologist who excavated Kahun between 1888 and 1890, discovered that almost every house had been invaded by rats and their holes had been stuffed with stones and rubbish. A pottery rat trap was also found. Cats were kept to protect food and grain from rodents but, in the absence of a cat, 'cat's grease' was recommended as a deterrent."

Mice do not want to be eaten and have altered their genetic coding for smell and sound just as have the cats—sort of an arms race. The smell of the fat signaled a cat was near and likely did act as a repellant. Perhaps the priests thought the fat contained a magical essence of the cat; we don't know for sure. Again, cat fat, fur licked by the cat (containing enzymes specific to the cat), and feces might, indeed, have worked as mouse repellents—again seeing that mice do not want to be eaten and evidence of cat presence would have obvious survival value.

The hair of the cat was used for burns:

A-portion-of-Cake
Hair-of-a-cat
Crush into one and apply thereto. (Bryan 2021, 69)

There was a substance called *kyphi* made by the ancient Egyptians for hundreds of years. It was mainly used as an incense, containing specific grasses and resins—the ingredients could change according to the preparer. Uses included odor control and disguising bad breath. The ancient Egyptians had bad teeth, brought about mainly from eating bread. Because of wind, bread would contain lots of sand grains and act as sandpaper on teeth, wearing them down and leading to abscesses, poor gums, and bad breath. Under a slightly different name, kyphi had other uses.

A variant recipe, called *Kapet,* takes us back into the field of the psychological effect of the drug, for here it is used to avert the harmful influence of gods, demons, and dead persons. The recipe not only calls for herbs and resins already mentioned, but it includes ingredients from what is in German aptly known as *Dreckapatheke* ("dirt pharmacy"), the excrement of the following creatures: lion, crocodile, swallow, gazelle, ostrich, and cat, as well as scorpion poison, donkey's hair, barbel of *Synodontis* catfish, and deer horn (Manniche 1999, 55).

Dreckapatheke, however, has been reevaluated, and it just might be the case that the ancient Egyptians were the first to make use of antibiotics.

[The ancient Egyptians] resorted to these mixtures chiefly in cases of the stubbornest types of trachoma and similar infections of the eye which defied other treatment. Urine was used for eyewash. Mud and soil were also employed in compresses. When Dr. Benjamin M. Dugger, Professor of Plant Physiology at the University of Wisconsin, presented the world in 1948 with the new drug Aureomycin, he certainly had no thought of his discovery upon our evaluation of Egyptian medicine.

It turned out that Aureomycin was highly effective in the treatment of trachoma. Aureomycin was the newest among the antibiotic "wonder drugs." It was extracted from a type of soil found particularly in the vicinity of cemeteries—and it was just one among some thirty thousand soil specimens Dugger and his colleagues had examined between 1944 and 1946. This soil produced fungi which had as annihilating an effect upon some disease bacteria as did the molds from which penicillin was derived.

Certain waste products that result from the metabolism of

these molds have an inhibiting effect on the growth of bacteria. Investigation soon showed that bacteria living in the human body release their excretory products into feces and urine, which therefore are rich in antibiotic substances.

We would be stretching the point to assert that the Egyptians were the discoverers of antibiotic drugs. Nevertheless, research into antibiotics led to a degree of caution in judging what had formerly been called "sewerage pharmacology."

Presumably the Egyptians originally included feces and urine in their "prescriptions because they expected these substances to drive out the demons which caused sickness. But then the substances suddenly produced successful cures—although in many cases they may only have done harm and produced new infections," since the Egyptians had no idea of their secret power. Success depended on chance. Nevertheless, especially in desperate cases, the "filth" worked wonders. Ultimately, the Egyptians developed a methodology for their use. The Ebers Papyrus alone contains as many as fifty-five prescriptions in which feces and urine are important components, for both external and internal use. (Thorwald 1963, 85–86)

One has to wonder where the inspiration for use of cat feces (and feces from other animals) as a healing medicine came from. Perhaps if the grain stored in silos was from the gods, and the mice ate the grain (a blessing from the gods), and the cats ate the mice, the priest-physicians, through analogous thinking, concluded that any part of the cat had healing powers, including excrement.

To continue, an important physical issue for ancient Egyptians was supple skin:

"To make everything possible supple" they had a wide choice of salves. One salve consisted of Flesh-of-the-Shadfish and Honey beaten up in Yeast-of-Sweet-Beer. Another salve with surely more claim to color than cure combined Writing-fluid, Vermilion, and Goat's Fat with Honey and several other ingredients, which were certainly only thrown in to make weight. In another salve Ass's dung reappears; it is combined with Yeast-of-the-Opium-drink, Goat's Fat, Lettuce, Onions, Beans, and White Oil. (Bryan 2021, 64–65)

Sometimes it was a pathological cause such as "hardening" which prevented the suppleness. In these cases, the "hardening" had to be gotten rid of first:

Salve to make supple the Hardening

Hog's Fat

Oil-of-Worms

Oil-of-the-abxersu-animal

Mouse Oil

Cat's Oil

Gather into one and anoint therewith. (Bryan 2021, 64–65)

For burns there were many remedies:

If one had more time there were other remedies that could be employed; for example, Elderberries and Papyrus-plant mixed in Gum-water and applied thereto. Or, if one preferred a dry remedy:

Another

A-portion-of-Cake

Hair of-a-Cat

Crush into one and apply thereto. (Bryan 2021, 68–69)

For dry skin we read:

For common scurf the ketket-plant and the Berry-of-the-uan-tree were ground into one with the Milk-of-a-woman, strained and drunk for four days. A simpler but hardly less pleasant remedy comprised equal parts of Sea-salt and Beer, which likewise had to be taken for four days. If the scurf was complicated by "Hardenings in all Limbs of a Person," heroic measures in the shape of a poultice composed of Pieces-of-excrement, Cat's dung, Dog's dung, and Berries-of-the-Xet plant were taken. "It drives out all the scurf," the Scribe added reassuringly. One devoutly hopes so. (Bryan 2021, 90)

For hardening of the stomach, we read:

TO DRIVE AWAY THE HARDENING IN THE ABDOMEN:
Bread-of-the-Zizyphus-Lotus
Watermelon
Cat's dung
Sweet Beer
Wine
Make into one and apply as a poultice. (Bryan 2021, 137)

To prevent baldness:

ANOTHER FOR THE GROWTH OF THE HAIR
ON A HEAD WHICH IS BECOMING BALD:
Fat-of-the-Lion
Fat-of-the-Hippopotamus
Fat-of-the-Crocodile
Fat-of-a-Cat
Fat-of-the-Serpent
Fat-of-the-Egyptian-Goat
Make into one and rub the head of the Bald one therewith.
(Bryan 2021, 153)

Leaving Egypt and going to Japan for a moment, the Japanese have an interesting use for cat skin. It is used to make a musical instrument called a *shamisen*, which is a banjo-like instrument. This is not a new or unique method of making musical instruments. Traditional American banjos are made of goat or calf skin, and the Moroccan sintir uses camel skin.

Stretched cat skin gives the instruments their resonance and sound. Even in modern Japan, shamisen are made from stretched cat skin, which has caused something of a dilemma. As cats are seen more as pets in modern Japan, people are unhappy with the idea of them being killed to make an instrument. Shamisen makers have experimented with alternate materials from plastic to kangaroo skin, but are forced to admit that only cat skins give shamisen their unique sound (Davisson 2021, 58–59).

Hopefully the reader will rethink the idea that cats were worshipped like gods. In order to obtain cat meat, fat, cat oil, or cat skin, one would need to kill the cat. No one would even think about using a god's skin for a banjo or oil of a god as a cosmetic. Food of the gods, yes, such as the symbolic consumption of Osiris's penis or the body of Christ during communion, but these are different metaphors entirely (Rush 2011, 2022). Also, cats on a diet of mice, other rodents, and a snake or two aren't likely to be fat cats. After dispatching and skinning the cat, any noticeable fat could be scraped off and rendered. Is this the proper manner in which to treat a god? No, it is not.

5

Issues of Cat Identity and Behavior in Spirituality

Our identity with cats, how we view cats in relation to ourselves, and other animals must go back at least to the time when we could articulate these identities, if not much earlier. This would, of course, have to coincide with the slow development of linguistic ability, of turning sounds and gestures into meaningful sentences and paragraphs. We can't be sure, but the idea of worshipping something must be relatively recent in hominin social evolution. Yes, our ancient ancestors were in awe of lightning and the power of big animals, but that is not worship.

CAVE ART AND SHAMANISM

One of the first identifiable animals many anthropologists claim was worshipped was the cave bear (*Ursus spelaeus*). The cave bear is a prominent image in cave paintings at the Chauvet cave site in France (dated to thirty-two thousand years ago), but because of climate change, its diet was disrupted by a decrease in temperature (not attributable to sinful humans) and it went extinct around twenty-four thousand years ago.*

---

*See Kurten 1976, which is informative but somewhat outdated, for more information on climate and extinction.

Recall how I defined worship earlier, that it is a supplicatory behavior, slavery to a deity and following its every dictate. It is unlikely the bear was worshipped, bowed down to, or communicated with in this manner; we did not follow the dictates of the bear. The bear was not, in my opinion, worshipped but was, instead, what we generally refer to as a shamanic-type instrument (nonhuman in this case)—dead, but still alive, used to commune with the other side to persuade the animals to come back for another meal. Of course, the animals were the meal but promises were made—the animals would be revered and remembered as they are magically drawn, transferring their spirit to cave walls indicating a sure return. What modern humans in Europe around fifty thousand years ago recognized, as did the Neanderthals for thousands of years before them, was that cave bears go down into the caves in the autumn and die (hibernate) and then are reborn in the spring, often with new life. The bear represents life, death, and return, the basic issues in most magico-religious systems. The bear was not a god, but these characteristics of the bear—a powerful animal that will stand on two legs (humanoid-like) and that dies and comes back to life—are interpreted as spiritual in that they allow passage to the other side, that other world, and communication with the forces that might be used or manipulated if the right words are spoken, rituals are performed, and the promise of immortality in our world is made through magical images in a cave. The caves were likely used in other ways, for rites of passage and other ritual observance, perhaps as cemeteries of sorts by painting the images of deceased clan members in the form of their animal totem, as astronomical references, and so on.

But the cave bear died out and ceased to come back for another meal, and all that was left were the bones—old bones—and this must have created a psychological crisis: how do we *now* contact the other side? This question was answered at the French cave sites of Lascaux (circa twenty-two thousand years ago) and Les Trois-Frères (seventeen thousand years ago). Certainly, these ancestors did not stay in psychological distress for two or three thousand years, and data is sparse at best to know how they handled this crisis. My position is (and it is only a guess) that the extinction of the bear was gradual and the group leaders who led the rituals, or who on occasion would risk life and limb to commune with the hibernating bear, likewise gradually and through analogous thinking took over where the bear left off. Our ancestors were becoming aware of their power and spiritual nature. At Chauvet there is a bear skull on a block of calcite that had fallen down from the ceiling or formed from an eroded stalagmite, along with around fifty other skulls in the surroundings. This indicates that communing with a *live* bear was probably rare; all that was necessary were parts of the body—the skulls in this case. The ritual use of those caves ended for some reason, perhaps due to weather changes and dispersal of groups to areas further south. About six to eight thousand years later (now twenty to twenty-two thousand years ago), a new cultural group moved into the area referred to as Solutreans. (We do not know what they called themselves.) At the cave sites of both Lascaux and Les Trois-Frères, we see the first evidence of the human animal as the conduit between this world and the other. The images are human but display animal traits, such as a bird at Lascaux (Thoth or Horus in ancient Egypt?) and a composite animal image at Les Trois-Frères made up of red deer antlers, wolf ears and tail, an owl's face, human body and legs, and the genitals of a male feline. The wolf and the feline were unlikely to be foodstuff and represent life (feline genitals) and death (the wolf), while the antlers of the red deer (foodstuff) represent the moon as the antlers fall off and regenerate, just as the moon sheds it shadow and is reborn. The owl, as a night predator, was likely a representation of the Underworld. Again, we don't know for sure if these symbolic values align with the thinking of these ancient people, but through comparison with modern groups we can intuit similarities.

For Lascaux, there are strong associations with cosmological issues, and although we don't know if they named obvious star clusters, the shaman with a bird's head (flying on mind-altering substances?) is to the left of a bison (Taurus), and in modern cosmology, Leo the lion sits above (Rappenglueck 2009). I will say more about cats and cosmology shortly. In any case, the shaman is *surrounded* by animals, all possibly signs in their zodiac, making him an animal master or even master of the cosmos (Magli 2009, 9–12).

The Sorcerer of Trois-Frères, on the other hand, *becomes* the animals by *wearing* their characteristics, similar to the leopard-skin chief and shamans in more recent times. One thing to keep in mind is that in all probability these ancient ancestors made little distinction between the animals they were hunting and eating and themselves. The idea of separating ourselves from nature, that is, nature being something separate (corrupt) from the human animal is a philosophy that had to wait many thousands of years. Monotheistic traditions tend to paint nature as separate, inferior, or even evil in order to "cleanse" themselves of polytheism, which, of course, they were never able to accomplish. We hear of the "nature religions," as commented on by Christian clerics, as inferior and lacking philosophy. But when you get right down to it, what else is there to worship but nature?

I recently asked an icon artist about the role of shamanism and the pagan traditions in Christian art, and she referred me to a priest who made the following comment on January 13, 2009:

The shaman analogy is, by comparison, quite a stretch. Shamans are understood to be precisely individuals who have acquired powers of influence over the natural order through a personal, life-changing experience of their own. The result is a special knowledge and a consequent "magical" potency. Certainly, they are concerned with the natural order (and an iconographer is also concerned with it), but *their religious perspective is animistic, not one derived from a highly developed (civilizational and philosophically influenced) religion.* The shaman's power is given him in order to manipulate the natural

order. He is viewed with awe and fear for his otherworldly powers, and he is considered unique and even dangerous. The iconographer, by contrast, is a humble, often anonymous, servant who
seeks to work in cooperation with God's grace, utilizing the materials that come from the redeemed creation. (Rush 2011, 281–82;
emphasis added)

The implication in this Anglican priest's conceptualization of shamanism is that Christianity is philosophical and connected to civilized
people and shamanism is not, which, of course, denies the Church's
humble origins.

Using the bear as a conduit between the two worlds suggests,
early on, a close identification with the characteristics of the bear
as well as other animals. An example would be the Lion-man, or
Löwenmensch figurine, discovered in Hohlenstein-Stadel (a German
cave) in 1939, dating to between thirty-five and forty thousand years
ago (Cook 2017). Although we don't know the thinking behind this
composite figurine, it would appear this is someone taking on the
characteristics of a lion, like strength and power, or it could be more
generic, representing the identity of a clan. It could also simply be a
toy carved for a child. In any case, as with the bear, it is the *characteristics* attributed to the animals that are captured in these renderings
and not worship of the animals proper.

Those ancient cave painters, who were likely shamans, might have
seen these caves as portals to the Underworld—modern humans apparently did not live in those dangerous caves, although Neanderthals
lived and buried their dead in some of them. We do not know how
these ancients viewed death, or even if the Underworld was important, but we don't encounter the idea of judgment at death. Those
caves were eventually abandoned, and after several thousand years we
begin to see, several thousand miles away in Samaria, in cuneiform
script, ideas about the Underworld. For the Sumerians it was a place,

in many cases, you simply went when you died—neither good nor bad. But there are suggestions, at least in our interpretation of the Solutrean images, that the person's soul went somewhere else, ideas that do not appear in the Sumerian metaphysics. These beliefs in a simple Underworld speak to the harsh life for the average agriculturist with no hope of relief. Making a living off the land was tough business complete with setbacks, that is, droughts, winds, and plant-destroying insects and rain. Today, you get a welfare check and go to the grocery store. For those ancient ancestors of 3000 BCE, if you didn't work and work hard, you didn't eat. Just imagine what our ancestors had to go through. Life expectancy, as you can imagine, was short, perhaps on the average of twenty-five to twenty-seven years for women and around thirty to thirty-five years for men.

Be that as it may, it is not until recent times* that we encounter the Underworld as a bad place for bad people.

WRITING AND EARLY CONCEPTS OF THE CAT

Images can reveal a great deal about a subject, but writing helps to fill in the details. The ancient Sumerians saw the Underworld as a dark, dank cavern, deep in the earth, and the only nourishment was provided by surviving relatives who would leave food and pour water on the ground over the grave site. After a few generations the deceased were forgotten and ended up in later traditions as hungry ghosts, *dim* or demons in the Mesopotamian mythology. Here we find, emerging from the subconscious, the fear of predator cats, but now they take on human characteristics, which may be a continuation of beliefs surrounding the Lion-man. The most dangerous animal in the world is another human being; humans can be monsters. Recall Hitler or Stalin—there is a long list of these elites torturing and murdering innocent people as I write this.

---

*See Bernstein 1993 for the evolution of modern conceptions of hell.

From the Mesopotamian tradition we hear of *lilītu* borrowed into the Hebrew tradition as Lilith. The following comes from the Jewish Virtual Library ("Lilith"):

> In the writings of Hayyim Vital (*Sefer ha-Likkutim* [1913], 6b), Lilith sometimes appears to people in the form of a cat, goose, or other creature, and she holds sway not for eight days alone in the case of a male infant and 20 for a female (as recorded in the *Alphabet of Ben Sira*), but for 40 and 60 days respectively. In the Kabbalah, influenced by astrology, Lilith is related to the planet Saturn, and all those of a melancholy disposition—of a "black humor"—are her sons (Zohar, *Ra'aya Meheimna* III, 227b). From the 16th century it was commonly believed that if an infant laughed in his sleep it was an indication that Lilith was playing with him, and it was therefore advisable to tap him on the nose to avert the danger. (H. Vital, *Sefer ha-Likkutim* (1913), 78c; *Emek ha-Melekh*, 130b)

The cat is mentioned several times in the Talmud. The Jewish book of law refers to the cat as having magical powers, especially the ability to see demons. Humans can borrow this ability by burning the placenta of a first-born female cat and placing a small amount of the powder in one's eye—demons will then become visible. In one Hebrew legend God asked a cat how it obtained food and the cat replied, "Give me my daily bread from an absent-minded woman who leaves her kitchen door open."

The cat is also connected to Lilith, Adam's first wife. Lilith wanted equality with Adam, which was denied, so she took up residence at the bottom of the Red Sea, from which she, at night, would make sport of sleeping males, bringing forth demons. In Spain Lilith is called La Broosha, who would murder children in the night by sucking out their blood; children should never be left alone after birth. In one narrative, when a nurse left a mother and baby alone the mother had a dream of a black cat entering the bedroom. It took the child "and threw it out of the window to another cat. Horrified, the nurse realized that it had not been a dream because she could see from the window the cat carrying the baby in its mouth as it crossed a nearby field" (Vocelle 2013).

Stories in the Jewish tradition suggest some ambivalence regarding cats, with lots of distain for dogs, although dogs served a purpose. There are numerous references to the lion in the Old Testament, to be discussed shortly, but no mention of the domesticated cat, and, although the ancient Egyptians saw domesticated cats as useful (in medicine and for protecting stored grain—see chapter 4) this apparently did not rub off on those (likely the followers of Akhenaten or Akhenaten's older brother, Thutmose) who eventually made their way to Canaan, the promised land, and became the Israelites with whom we are familiar (Schwartz 2014).

Podwal (2021, 38) comments:

The very first law in the Shulehan Arukh, the code of Jewish law meant to guide the Jewish people through every facet of their lives, commands, "Arise like a lion to serve your creator in the morning" (1: 1). Crowned "king of beasts" by the Talmud (*Chagigah* 13b), the lion is the emblem of authority, strength, bravery, and majesty. The Hebrew Bible contains more than a hundred references to this royal beast, many metaphorical. Comparisons include the tribe of Judah, King David, Israel, the Temple, and even God. "Like as a lion . . . so will the Lord of Hosts come down to fight on Mount Zion," says the prophet Isaiah (31:4).

The lion is also the fifth sign of the zodiac (Leo), corresponding to the fifth Hebrew month, Av. *Yalkut Shimoni,* a thirteenth-century midrashic anthology, states that the lion* came in the month of the lion (Av) and destroyed the lion (the temple).

---

*Nebuchadnezzar is referred to in the book of Jeremiah as a lion.

It is said in the Talmud that the Roman emperor summoned Rabbi Joshua ben Hananiah to the royal palace and said to him, "Your God is likened unto a lion in your scriptures. But it is known that a strong man can kill a lion. So how mighty can your God be?" (Chullin 59b). Rabbi Joshua responded that the scriptures refer not to an ordinary lion but to a lion of the forest of Ilai. The emperor demanded to see the lion in question, and so Rabbi Joshua began to pray—and the lion came out of its den. When the lion was four hundred miles away, he began to roar. Frightened by the terrible sound, all the pregnant women in Rome miscarried, and the walls of Rome crumbled. When the lion was three hundred miles away, he roared again. All the teeth of the citizens of Rome fell out, and the emperor tumbled off his throne. The emperor then hurried to the house of Rabbi Joshua and said, "I asked you to pray that I may see the lion of the forest of Ilai. Now I beg you to pray that I never see him. Make him return to his forest" (Chullin 58b). Once more Rabbi Joshua began to pray. The lion of the forest of Ilai returned to his lair—whence, it is hoped, he will never emerge again.

In discussing special blessings instituted by the sages to be recited upon seeing extraordinary sights, the Gemara says that one who passes a lion's den recites "Blessed be He Who performed miracles for our ancestors in this place" (Talmud, Berakhot 54a) in remembrance of Daniel's miraculous emergence unscathed from a lion's den.

As mentioned, there are numerous entries in the Old and New Testaments referencing lions. One famous story is "Samson and Delilah," perhaps a reference to the "strong man" mentioned above. As the story goes (Judges 13–14, New International Version), Samson's mother, simply referred to as "Manoah's wife," is unable to have children (like Sarah, Abraham's wife). God fixes it up and a prophecy is rendered stating that Samson will be the "hand of the Lord until he dies." Samson is born, and later he meets a Philistine woman and falls madly in love ("Oh no! Not a Philistine!" The Philistines were ruling over Israel at the time, and there was understandable hostility). While with his parents on the way back from meeting his future in-laws, a young lion jumps out (I can still see Victor Mature beating up a poor drugged lion, in the 1949 movie, *Samson and Delilah*). He kills the lion, time passes, and on his way back to Delila, he goes past the lion and sees bees and honey in the lion's abdomen. He scoops up some of the honey and honeycomb and enjoys a "snack" on the way to the party. He marries Delilah and is hanging out with the Philistines, feasting away, when a riddle is offered with a stake of thirty linen garments to the winner—if the Philistines lose, then they must give Samson thirty linen garments and vice versa.

> *Out of the eater, something to eat;*
> *out of the strong, something sweet.*
>
> (JUDGES 14:14,
> NEW INTERNATIONAL VERSION)

This is where we get into the female's ability to tempt—sort of a play on Eve "tempting" Adam: Delilah's coaxing of Samson to answer the riddle for her, the hair cutting (hair is magical in many cultures) and loss of his strength, and the betrayal and blinding as he doesn't have the strength to defend himself. (As an aside, Delilah would not have the ability to tempt if men weren't programmed to be tempted.)

Sampson's magical hair grows back. He destroys the Philistine temple, lots of Philistines die, and God is pleased. What is this all about, especially the lion? The lion represents the obvious things: strength and power. But God has given Samson a great power: power over the animals, lions included, making Samson a shaman of sorts. The lion will certainly eat you, as symbolized by the lion's initial aggression toward Samson, and, of course, some Christians were thrown to the lions along with many others, both criminals and innocents. The lion is also a symbol of the sun, for just as the sun pounces on the moon, the lion pounces on the bull, and then the sun rises for another day. The original meaning was a characteristic of God (sun), that is, powerful and perhaps wrathful. The killing of the lion was just a hint as to how Samson would eventually utilize the power of God. Killing the lion was, in this case, a metaphor for destroying the Temple of Dagon, the god of the Philistines, at Ras Shamra, the gates of which are guarded by two colossal lions.

But there is another meaning here involving the bees and the honey and their connection to mind-altering substances. According to Ruck et al. (2007, 302), making comparisons between "mead" (not necessarily a fermented drink made from honey), bees, honey, and intoxicating substances:

> Thus, there can be little doubt that the bee phenomenon and its intoxicating honey are a trans-global archetype. Bees are souls, messengers of the gods; the swarm indicates the presence of divinity and the hum of their buzzing describes the ecstatic communion with them; the theft of the honeycomb is synonymous with the ascent up the Cosmic Axis and the experience of the bear's hibernating shamanic trance; the honeycomb is metaphoric for the sacramental food.

The sacred food, according to Ruck, is *Amanita muscaria,* the sacred mushroom. Be that as it may, lions are also connected to resurrection:

> When the lion sleeps, it keeps its eyes open and watches. The lion sleeping with its eyes open represents Christ on the cross; his body sleeps in death, but his divinity keeps watch at the right hand of God. The second property is that the lion cub is born dead, but is brought to life after three days when the father breathes on its face (some accounts say the father roars over the cub). This represents Christ's three days in the grave, after which God his father revived him. (Badke 2004)

We also find in Isaiah 11: 6–9 (New International Version):

The wolf will live with the lamb,
the leopard will lie down with the goat,
the calf and the lion and the yearling together;
and a little child will lead them.
The cow will feed with the bear,
their young will lie down together,
and the lion will eat straw like the ox.
The infant will play near the cobra's den,
and the young child will put its hand into the viper's nest.
They will neither harm nor destroy
on all my holy mountain,
for the earth will be filled with the knowledge of the LORD
as the waters cover the sea.

What is the meaning here? The reference is to heaven, paradise, and the Garden of Eden. In that place, the Garden of Eden, everything and nothing is happening at the same instant, but there is no time, a characteristic of the waveform in quantum physics (chapter 7). Our hero, Eve, said no to God's dictates, decided that the Tree of Knowledge would be good for humans, and ate the "fruit" (a mushroom, I might add—see Rush 2022), woke up, and, along with Adam, was thrown out of the Garden "lest they become *like* us," although we are told the expulsions occurred because they disobeyed God. Any knowledge gained in the Garden serves no purpose; it is only by leaving the garden and entering the field of time that the knowledge becomes useful. In quantum physics, the Garden would represent the waveform, and once observed (being outside the Garden) the physical world comes into play. All the knowledge of the universe resides in the waveform but is not usable or functional until it is observed by a lifeform in the field of time. In the biblical narrative, knowledge is accessed through the "fruit" of the Tree of Knowledge, once *outside* the Garden. So God had to get Adam and Eve out of the Garden if life is to play a part in the universe he created, and the "fruit" of the Tree of Knowledge was a way to get back in.

Back to the lion and the lamb, the lion or the leopard will eat the lamb and the small child, but not now because nothing is happening. Time stands still in the Garden of Eden (because there is no time), there is nothing good, nothing evil; there is only information in the form of codes. That duality, those qualities of good and evil, is only available if you leave and enter the field of life (time), a choice Eve made for us, and she has been condemned for choosing knowledge over God ever since. At some point in our evolution we woke up and realized that although we are part of nature, we can step back and appreciate the good, the bad, and the ugly. We, in a sense, become the gods. That cannot happen in the biblical Garden of Eden until you break the law, eat the "fruit," and jump into the mist. In the Garden of Eden, we could only be *similar* (as in "like") to the gods; in the field of time we can *become* the gods, and we do this by going into the waveform, extracting information, and returning.

As the story goes, Adam has a third son, Seth, to replace Able who, as you recall, was murdered by his brother Cain. Seth, it should be noted, is the connection many Gnostic groups point back to in their celestial genealogy. In any case, Adam is about to pass into that celestial geography far, far away, and he summons Seth to his side and requests that he travel to the Garden of Eden and obtain three seeds from the fruit of the Tree of Life (either immortality or knowledge, as they both represent life). But this is easier said than done. As you may recall from your Sunday school lessons, after Adam and Eve were thrown under the bus, God stationed a seraph with a very large sword at the gates of paradise. Well, when Seth reached the gate, he was allowed to pass; apparently only Adam and Eve were restricted from the Garden in this original story. But there is a price to pay, for the seraph will baptize with fire (the mushroom, perhaps?). Seth went through the gates, through the fire of the Seraph, and was immediately captivated by the sights and sounds, the colors and melodies that rippled from each leaf, blade of grass, rock, or pond. Finally Seth found the tree in the shape of horns, glowing red, with spotted fruits on its branches and on the ground below. He was cautioned about lingering in this place "because of the beauty," his father told him. Then there was Snake, awakening after a long sleep. Opening one eye and standing on her tail, she followed Seth's path to the tree. "Take the biggest ones without trouble and leave the rest," spoke Snake. Seth turned to retrace his steps, while Snake closed her eye, smiled, and went into a long, deep sleep. Seth hastened his step because he realized the Garden of Eden is the pause, the time between time, where the lion sleeps with the lamb. Pausing too long would trap the individual in an endless nothingness and upon return one would find that much time had passed.

Seth returned to the grove of trees and found Adam in final repose, placed the fruits in his mouth, and buried him in the center. Many years passed and from Adam's grave grew three Lebanese cedars from which the three crosses on Golgotha were fashioned (Rush 2022, 272–73).

I have more to say about quantum physics, dreams (cats and human), and visiting the waveform in chapter 7.

From the Greek and Roman traditions, we encounter the chimera, which stands for illusion and fantasy, a mixture of ingredients forming a symbol of mystery and danger. The beast also speaks to treacherous territories with volcanoes and such.

The chimera is one of the most fearsome monsters from Greek mythology. The beast is understood to be female, although she is depicted with a mane like a male lion. The word "chimerical" has come to describe any implausible composite of dissimilar things. Most classical renderings portray this lion-like monster as three-headed with a goat's head growing from the middle of her back and a snake's head at the end of her tail. Yet the chimera had only one head in her earliest known descriptions, in Homer's *Iliad*. She was said to have the front half of a lion, the hindquarters of a she-goat, and the tail of snake. In all descriptions, the chimera is fire-breathing and nearly impossible to defeat.

In the *Iliad*, King Lobates attempted to dispose of a young man named Bellerophon by assigning him to slay the chimera. But Bellerophon was too smart to try to confront the beast like an ordinary foe. He consulted the Oracle and then tamed the legendary Pegasus. The flying horse allowed Bellerophon to hurl his spear down the chimera's throat. The lead spear melted inside the monster's fiery maw, sealing up her windpipe and killing her. This epic battle supposedly took place on a volcano in Lycia, Anatolia. The volcano was referred to as Mount Chimera by the Romans. The Roman scholar Servius speculated that the volcano itself was the monstrous chimera. He wrote that it has lions near its top, goats at the middle level, and snakes at its base. The volcano is fictional but is thought to have been inspired by a Lycian natural gas vent called Yanartaş (Frigiola 2019, 53–54).

The lion also shows up in Christian art. The lion is the determinative for St. Mark of Gospel fame; along with the human, ox, and eagle, the lion was borrowed from the heads on the canopic jars (New Kingdom 1600 BCE–1050 BCE) that held the various internal organs of the individual being mummified. The New Kingdom canopic jars have heads that represent the four sons of Horus and they protect the deceased as they are positioned at the four points of the compass in the tomb. When the Catholic Church was constructing their narrative they borrowed in the four sons of Horus who became Matthew, Mark, Luke, and John. But the lion is Mark's otherworldly condition, the *power* to capture words (truth) for eternity.

However, in the Book of Kells we encounter the lion symbolic of "something else":

The Book of Kells is an Irish manuscript transcribed by Christian monks sometime around 800 CE, but the work itself spans the sixth to the ninth centuries. Now at Trinity College in Dublin, Ireland, this manuscript lay in the abbey in Kells, County Heath, Ireland, for many centuries. It includes the New Testament Gospels and obviously reflects Jesus as human and God. Ornately illustrated in

Celtic design, the mystery is easily disguised in the illustrious art. One finds swirling serpents and mythical monsters, which suggest that the "other side" can be a dangerous place. One also notes the facial expressions, suggesting trance or deep meditation. There are 340 folios or pages bound in four volumes. (Rush 2022, 176–77)

The lion referred to above is to be found on Folio 29R of the Book of Kells:

Another favorite is Folio 29R (Plate 2, 25), which comes from Matthew 1, table of the descent of Christ, indicating genealogical connections. Notice the "lion" to the right of Matthew at the top center. It has a mushroom cap halo and is partaking of the Eucharist in the form of a mushroom; the Eucharist is the body of Christ, and Christ and/or Jesus is the mushroom. I have heard that the lion is, instead, a monster, but a monster partaking of the holy fungus would simply bring forth more monsters—the mind-set of a monster is not the mind-set for bringing forth Jesus. If you look closely the lion has a halo composed of the circle with red and white spots. This may be the lion in Revelation and the Eucharist is the seventh seal. Each of the seven seals represents a ritual that might indicate a type of substance and how much of a substance to administer. (Rush 2022, 181)

CATS AND THE ITALIAN WITCH

Returning to the activities of Lilith mentioned in connection to Jewish beliefs, I conducted a very lengthy study of magic and witchcraft beliefs held by many in the Italian community of Toronto; some of the data was published in the early 1970s.* Italian metaphysics has

---

*For more information see my book *Witchcraft and Sorcery: An Anthropological Perspective of the Occult* (1974).

a long season, the construction of which dates many hundreds if not thousands of years prior to Christianity. Elements of this composite tradition can be seen in Celtic, Etruscan, Greek, and Middle Eastern myths and narratives.

The poverty in southern Italy allowed for the maintenance of such beliefs, syncretized in Catholicism, as there was and is great suspicion of those in power. Shunning the medical community, except for veterinarians and perhaps a medical student in the family, meant that the majority of medical issues—from birthing to physical maladies and curses—were handled by a *fattuchiera* (*magi* in northern Italy), better known as a sorceress. (There was a male counterpart, a "bone setter" (*conciaossa*), but my research did not reveal any information about such a person). During our stay in Rome we noted that doctor's offices and hospitals were not all that obvious; herbal shops, on the other hand, were very common and staffed by knowledgeable herbalists. We also noted that disabled individuals, people in wheelchairs as we see in this country, were not all that visably, either. Inquiring about this we were simply told, "We can't afford them." This will give the reader some idea about poverty in southern Italy and the necessity of maintaining older traditions; they cannot afford medical doctors.

The word *fattuchiera* is related to the noun *fattura* (curse) as many illnesses and accidents were considered the product of curses, most importantly coming from the "evil eye" (*malocchio*) or simply the "look." People are powerful and anyone can curse—especially through envy. To verbally express envy, such as "What a beautiful child," without following it with *"Dio benedict"* ("God bless") places a curse on the subject of envy. A stranger envying people and possessions is especially troublesome because that individual is probably a witch. Witches usually injure and kill with curses and touch, while werewolves (another strong symbol in Italian culture long before the influence of modern cinema) injure and kill violently. Our small-group nature primes us for suspicion of outsiders, strangers, and those cats of past ages. Strangers are unpredictable; our behavior changes when around strangers, and rightly so. Also programmed in our genes is deception,* and this is generally accomplished both verbally and through body language. We know that we deceive and, through projection, outsiders are suspect.

To continue, stone masons were needed in the Toronto area at the beginning of twentieth century, and the call went out to the world. It was answered by many men from southern Italy, who migrated to Toronto, found work, and merged with the dominant culture. After a year or so they would send for family members: wife, children, and so on. The men, out of necessity, learned English and many of the "native" customs, including medical practices. When the women were brought over they became encapsulated in "Little Italy," while the children were required to go to school. The children, like the men, had a foot in each world. The older women maintained their traditions, and sometimes these beliefs and practices passed to their daughters. This migration to Toronto, and the laws encountered, restricted the behavior of the fattuchiera, and a great deal of information was lost and not transmitted to the next generation. What I encountered was only a small part of the original beliefs and practices.

There were two types of sorcerers in the Italian community of Toronto: good sorcerers, who applied the traditional brand of healing, and evil sorcerers, unknown of course, who did evil deeds like casting spells and so on. Then there were witches, who, according to folk legends, followed good sorcerers to Toronto from the Old World because they aided in preventing or canceling the evil deeds of specific witches. (Apparently werewolves did the same.) Like the evil sorcerers, no one really knew who the witches were, but in Toronto, unlike the small village in Italy where they grew up, these immigrants were

---

*Cats, dogs, birds, and other animals also practice deception; for more about this, see my book *Clinical Anthropology: An Application of Anthropological Concepts with Clinical Settings* (1996).

by this time *surrounded* by strangers, many of whom were likewise Italian. For example, one should avoid old women dressed in black (mourning clothes), for she could be a witch in disguise. This is likely the origin of the witch wearing black clothing.

Witches could injure or kill through touch but were considered shape-shifters, doing most of their dirty work in the form of a rat or cat, the cat being the most favored. Like in the Jewish tradition, babies should never be left alone. I heard numerous stories of cats jumping into baby carriages and biting a baby or licking the dried milk off a baby's lips and smothering the child; SIDS (Sudden Infant Death Syndrome) needed an explanation and cats were convenient. It is difficult to untangle the ancient beliefs about cats and those fostered by the Catholic Church, but certainly a black cat should be avoided lest it is a witch in disguise. The witch hunt craze in medieval Europe undoubtedly helped to reinforce any negative ancient beliefs the Italian curers had regarding black cats in particular. But there is another part to the story.

When sorcerers get sick, an explanation is needed, for they should be able to cure themselves. The explanation is the witch, much the same as we blame the unseen modern witches, cancer, bacteria, and viruses (such as COVID-19 and its variants). During a personal conversation she had with me on May 18, 1970, one very famous sorceress related that she was quite effective in removing difficult curses, yet had difficulty when she ran up against a witch who cursed her:

> . . . [C]urses from the malocchio from people, sometimes innocently, these are easy to remove. But that of a witch, she has powers I do not have. She is of the other side; I can only visit. She is born evil. I offended one in particular. She used to come to me in my dreams, threatening, and there was always a cat involved, her companion, her double. When I came to Toronto, I thought it was over, but she followed me. Our spirits crossed in a dream of a canyon I fell into, in a strange place next to the ocean, and I heard a voice, *"Ti ho trovato"*

["I found you"]; it was her. She knew my name and I didn't know her name. I called her, *Nasone,* but that wasn't it. And here I am cursed by nasone ("big nose").

Mae (not her real name) died about one year after this interview from liver failure, and I was one of the pallbearers at her funeral. This was a sad day as she had helped many in the kindred; she never turned anyone away. I will have more to say about "spirits crossing in a dream" in chapter 6.

The Italian witch (*strega*), then, just as shape-shifting Lilith, uses her power in destructive ways, one of which is murdering children while they sleep; some researchers see Lilith as the empress of hell.

Sometime between the ancient Sumerians of 3500 BCE and the Assyrians of 1000 BCE the Underworld became a place of judgment, a method or threat for maintaining social mores. I am puzzled as to why there wasn't a judgmental Underworld early on for the Sumerians, as certainly the ancient Egyptians had a judgmental Underworld as evidenced in the Pyramid Texts carved into the pyramid of Unas around 2400 BCE, with sentiments likely predating this by many hundreds of years.

In any case, the Underworld becomes a place of judgment. You have done evil things and so you must endure those evils in hell, a celestial threat. In ancient Egypt, for example, the Underworld* was a place of judgment as previously stated, but it could be traversed if proper rites and rituals were performed, similar to but much more elaborate than the last rites given by the Catholic Church. The cat persona in the ancient Egyptian context of the Underworld becomes a gate guardian of both the Upper and Lower Worlds symbolized as the lion, the guardian of the Two Lands—that is Upper and Lower Egypt, as well as the Upper World and the Underworld.

---

*In Egypt the Underworld had many names: Duat, Tuat, Tuaut, Amenti, Amenthes, Akert, and Neter-khertet (Rush 2007).

Power is one of the major attributes of the cat, in large manner this resulting from their physical characteristics, and it is through these physical characteristics that our ancestors imagined an attachment to the spiritual realm. But in reverse we admired that power, wanting to take it for ourselves, and we did this symbolically with animal teeth (making stone tools or jewelry), animal skins, clan names, and paintings on cave walls. The attribution of human characteristics to animals is what anthropologists call anthropomorphism, like that of mice (Mickey Mouse), dogs (Goofy), coyotes (Wile E. Coyote), rabbits (Bugs Bunny), cats (Sylvester and Garfield), and so on. For many years anthropologists and others were warned that attributing human characteristics to nonhuman animals was not scientific. I disagree. All animals share the same basic neurologic structures (See Shubin's *Your Inner Fish* PBS series, or Shubin 2020), and for my purposes I will confine my discussion to mammals. Your cat or dog has the same basic neurologic structures as we do, although the cerebral cortex (the gray matter) is much reduced. The limbic system and the contributing structures are very much the same, and this being so, we can expect they have similar emotions and basic behaviors connected to emotions. Moreover, a cat has a light sensitive pineal gland, as do humans (as well as your dog and other mammals); this is thought of as the "third eye" noted on the forehead of Shiva, the destroyer god, part of the trinity of Life, Death, and Return in the Hindu tradition. So to suggest that mammals are completely different from us in terms of emotions and behaviors places humans in some category above and beyond other mammals. I think this is a false assumption and a product of wishful thinking. But in the case of the cat (and other powerful animals), this attribution works in reverse, that is assigning animal characteristics to humans or human-like entities. We fashion the gods after ourselves and our experiences—the energy that informs all usually comes with a face, and that face informs us about the characteristics of, for example, the cat. Examples of this would be the Lion-man and Sekhmet, the goddess usually displayed with a human female body and a lion's head; this is likewise the case for Tefnut (water or mist) connected to the initial act of creation (Gadalla 2018).

In the Litany of Re, Re is described as "The One of the Cat" and as "The Great Cat." The nine realms of the universe are manifested in the cat; for both the cat and the Grand Ennead (meaning nine-times unity) share the same ancient Egyptian term *b.st* (Bastet). This relationship has found its way to Western culture, where one says that the cat has nine lives (realms) (Gadalla 2017, 110).

The cat in this case, likewise, is not a god but symbolic of the energy that informs the universe. The major characteristic of the cat is POWER. The "nine realms" (or ennead) in Egyptian cosmology is composed of Re (or Atum as creator), Shu (air, heat), Tefnut (mist, water), Geb (earth god), Nut (sky goddess), Osiris (fertility or life, judge of the Dead), Isis (life, nurturing, or spiritual qualities), Seth (evil, the unknown), and Nephthys (carnal or animal nature, mistress of the household).

Although we don't know in the Lion-man's case, a best guess, comparing it to the known characteristics of Sekhmet and Tefnut, is that the lion represents power, likely *shamanic* power. In reviewing Gaelic folklore, Forbes (2018, 76) might be addressing a connection to the Lion-man statue of thirty to forty thousand years ago:

In Scottish myths, R. C. Maclagan says that cat just signifies cat, also in its modern aspirated form "cath," a tribe, a battalion, according to O'Reilly, 3000 men. Connected with it is the Latin *caterra*, a hoop, and most probably *Ceatharn*, a troop, in Scottish Gaelic, and *ceatharnach*, a trooper, a stout, robust man, a soldier, a *cateran*, a "kern" as Sir Walter Scott has it. A cat-headed battalion is referred to on page 77 (English) of the Book of the *chait*, or Carbar of the cat's head, from wearing the skin on his casque or helmet. In the yellow book of Lecan, as in Revue Celtique, Tome IX, warriors with cat's heads upon them are mentioned, one being a Gaelic champion "of the men of the Gael" in particular. Lady Gregory gives an account of cat-headed men, which Fionn fought and destroyed. An ancient Irish poem, "Tale son of Trone," i.e., Tale mae Troon or Treun, Tale of the son of the firm or mighty, is called the cat-headed chief from the same reason, having had the armour of his head entirely covered in the skin of a wild cat, which made the knight appear as if he had a cat's head. Among northern nations the cat was sacred to the Goddess Frea.

Frea, Freya of Norse mythology, is connected to love, sex, and war (triplism), and she rides around in a war chariot pulled by two cats. The cat is not worshipped but, instead, used as a magical beast of burden.

The cat men noted by Forbes were warriors, again exploiting symbols of the cat's power and perhaps cunning in warfare. The "cat-headed chief" might allude to shamanic power, but that is not clearly stated. Myths, especially if they touch a chord (archetypes, if you are a good Jungian), are difficult to eradicate although they may transform over time. I have not uncovered evidence of warfare in Germany thirty to forty thousand years ago (feuds may have occurred), so I am not sure if Lion-man is representative of a warrior. He is more likely a shaman, but the connection to power is obvious. I'm not sure many of us would approach warfare dressed as a rabbit, any more than a football team would refer to themselves as the Chicken Raiders, although we do have the Anaheim Ducks ice hockey teams.

CHARACTERISTICS OF CATS

The following represent biological and behavioral characteristics of cats that are seen in various cultures as spiritual. These categories overlap but will be considered individually. I find it very interesting and telling that the cat seems more memorable in myths and folklore than the dog, "man's best friend." Conway (2021, 55–56) presents an extensive list of mythic cats from various cultures, some of which are mentioned below.

POWER

Cats are powerful animals—pound for pound much more powerful than the human animal. With powerful leg muscles, some cats, like the house cat or leopard, can jump onto tree branches many feet past the length of the animal. In South Africa, it was the leopards who could snatch one of our Australopithecine cousins and drag him or her up a tree, out of reach of the much heavier lions and other predators and where the tree branches and leaves would protect from the prying eyes of buzzards and such. Trees grow out of cave openings—that is where the moisture is, and it is in cave sites in South Africa, such as Sterkfontein, Swartkrans, Kromdraai, and Taung, that we have found the bones of many of our ancient bipedal cousins. Countless bones are found chewed up and deposited in these caves due to the rather messy eating habits of leopards. Just image, if you will, the stress these ancestors were under—all of them—for millions of years. The leopards were stressed as well—they needed to eat.

An example of power and the ferocious use of that power is to be found in Sekhmet as mentioned earlier—the lion-headed goddess usually connected to earlier times in ancient Egypt and the most common and visible cat in the beginning Egypt's history. She has a female human body with a lion's head. This is not in any way worship of a lion but worship of the goddess with *characteristics* of a lion.

As the story goes, Amun-Re was unhappy that humans were neglecting him and not paying proper respect. He felt rejected and puzzled, for he provided light and life, riding the heavens during the day and defeating cosmic evil during his night journey. He informed his daughter, Hathor, about the situation, and in a rage, she morphed into Sekhmet and began to devour human kind. After puffing out his chest and exclaiming "I'll show them who's boss," he reflected and said, " . . . but if she eats them all, who will worship me?"

With that he acquired several barrels of beer, colored red by Egyptian henbane added to the brewing process, and poured the alcohol/hallucinogenic mix on the ground. Sekhmet, thinking it was human blood, drank up the liquid and fell into a deep, deep sleep. With that Amun-Re puffed out his chest again saying, "I've saved humanity; what a good boy am I!"

Sekhmet exhibited the power and ferocity of the lion; again, this is not worship of the lion, but a *determinative* or adjective describing Sekhmet's potential. Anytime a deity comes with a lion's head you know the reference is to Sekhmet—with exceptions being Maahes or Mahes, the ancient lion-headed god of war, said to be the son of either Bastet or Sekhmet (Wilkinson 2003, 178) and Tefnut, mentioned earlier. The deity is not the lion but simply represents the ferocious characteristics of the lion. An interesting twist on power found in many mythologies is when power used for evil purposes is captured for use by humans to protect themselves or to defeat one's enemies. Amun-Re, for example, uses the lion, a determinative for Sekhmet, to punish humans for disobedience. We also read in *The Leyden Papyrus* (Griffith and Thompson 1974, 57) a threat to the gods and a divining lamp, and using the fury of Sekhmet the author or healer even threatens the oil lamp if demands are not met:

> Speak, Isis, let it be told to Osiris concerning the things which I ask about, to cause the god to come in whose hand is the command, and give me answers to everything about which I shall inquire here today. When Isis said "Let a god be summoned to me that I may send him," he being discrete as to the business on which they are brought to her; thou art the lamp was brought to her. The fury of Sekhmet thy mother and Heke thy father is cast at thee, thou shalt not be lighted for Osiris and Isis, thou shalt not be lighted for Anubis until

thou have given me an answer to everything which I ask about here to-day truly without telling me falsehood. If thou wilt not do it, I will not give thee oil.

One of the characteristics of Re in the Underworld was actually Re in the form of a long-eared cat slaying the monster serpent, Apophis. An example is the mural from the tomb of Inkerkhau in Twentieth Dynasty Egypt (u/Historian 2018). Here we see the power of the cat symbolically utilized by Re as he navigates the Underworld.

Re, in his sun boat, traverses the heavens during the day, from east to west on the back of Nut, the sky goddess, symbolic of the Milky Way. In the evening he is swallowed by Nut and then navigates through the Underworld, where he encounters Apepi or Apophis, the symbol of cosmic evil, at which point he morphs into a cat, slitting the monster's throat and emerging in the dawn unscathed as Re, the newborn sun, through Nut's vagina.

Unlike in the Jewish-Christian tradition, in ancient Egypt creation was not a one-time event but was repeated each day thereafter with the rising of the sun. The appropriate rituals must be performed if the sun is to rise. This cycle represents life, death, and return, a common theme in religious traditions, and represents psychological protection from the finality of death. The story is an echo of that connected to the cave bear of Paleolithic times.

Another example of power in the Egyptian tradition, power over life and death, involves the Opening of the Mouth Ceremony, presided over by the leopard-skin chief. This ritual, noted graphically in the Book of the Coming Forth by Light (also known as the Book of the Dead prepared, as an example, for Ani, an obviously wealthy Theban scribe), allowed the deceased to open his mouth and speak, know his name,* the names of

---

*You exist as a name or number in modern society, and without name or number you do not exist.

the monsters guarding the twelve gates, and be able to give his Negative Confession to forty-two judges. Knowing a monster's name, for example, Rumpelstiltskin, allows one power over the monster, or at least to be able to keep evil at bay. If demons, like government agencies, do not know your name or number, they cannot pursue, prosecute, or incarcerate.

The Negative Confession for the Egyptians, that is, "I do not lie, I do not cheat, I do not take grain from the temple silos, I do not kill . . ." represents statements of *personal responsibility,* something sorely lacking in modern society. There are forty-two confessions, one for each of the forty-two judges. If a judge detects truth he says *"Maa Kheru"* or "True of voice/action" (Gadalla 2018, 194).

The confessor, I must add, has previously engaged a ritual so that his or her heart won't betray the individual if telling a lie—the ancient Egyptians thought you *thought* with your heart. The Negative Confession is delivered in front of scales that weigh the confessor's heart against a feather (the heart has to weigh less than the feather); the scales are attended by Ma'at (cosmic law), Thoth (who writes it all down), and the female composite monster Ammut, who is waiting for a meal. Ammut is composed of a crocodile head, a lion's front end, and the rear end of a hippopotamus. A person not passing the test of the forty-two judges is given to Ammut, who eats the person's heart; that person is thus left in limbo forever. Have you ever heard the phrase "Eat your heart out"? Well, this is where it came from. The confessor who passes the test receives a name change, common in many cults or religious traditions; for example, Osiris Ani, and he is then led by Horus to Osiris: "Osiris is going to Osiris; I and the father are one."

As mentioned, the confessor has previously performed a ritual so that his or her heart won't betray whether they tell a lie. Just the same, this is quite different from the Ten Commandments wherein you are *told* what to do. Personal responsibility smacks of independent decision-making as well as the importance of the individual, a very different philosophy than that coming from most Middle Eastern countries to this day, but this is similar to the hunter-gatherer traditions of Europe. Perhaps there is a close but ancient connection between ancient Egypt and the hunter-gatherers who built Göbekli Tepe thousands of years before (Collins 2018). In any case, an example of differences between the Egyptian Negative Confession and the Ten Commandments is personal responsibility. In Middle Eastern philosophy, we encounter the opposite of personal responsibility and the *insignificance* of the individual in the story of Job in the Old Testament. Job is treated very badly by demon Yahweh, and although in need of an explanation for his treatment, he bows down to the demon's power, just as he would bow down to the king. Even today, in the magical thinking espoused in Marxist philosophy, the individual and personal incentive are of little importance. Marxist philosophy is a return to kingship, rule by the elite, feudalism, and the magical thinking that through violence you can create utopia.*

In the above example of weighing the heart against the feather, Ani, for whom a Book of the Dead was prepared, passes the test and is welcomed by Osiris into the Field of Reeds. The deceased were called Westerners because they travel west (many of the Egyptian tombs are located on the west side of the Nile), and it occurred to me that the "Field of Reeds" might refer to an earlier "Garden of Eden," the lush lakes, marshes, and grasslands in the Libyan Desert that existed prior to 5600 BCE. Global warming (beginning around 9600 BCE) also resulted in the flooding of the Black Sea basin and what is now the area of the Persian Gulf around 5600 BCE. When we speak of the Garden of Eden, in my opinion, there were many garden spots, the Libyan Desert possibly being one of them. Again, the global warming that began around 9600 BCE, at the end of that mini ice age, the Younger Dryas, likely caused the flooding in about 5600 BCE that

---

*Marxism, by the way, has nothing to do with the comedy trio, The Marx Brothers, a common mistake.

was mentioned in the Gilgamesh epic of Sumerian fame and is also likely the origin of the flood story in the Bible.

Returning to the leopard-skin chief, he is a person with power, representing a general characteristic of the leopard. He has the power to perform the ceremony, essentially power of life over death—in this case death in the now and life in the spiritual realm. From the Sorcerer of Trois-Frères (16,000 BCE) and the leopard-skin chief who is prominent at Çatalhöyük, Turkey circa 7100–5700 BCE (Mellaart 1965; Hodder 2006) to ancient Egypt, we note that the individuals wearing the leopard skin had the power not just to settle disputes as suggested by Evans-Prichard (1940), but power over life and death. The Sorcerer of Trois-Frères is an example of an early shaman, the animal master, who had power over the animals—really the cosmos. Again, we see the same shamanic behavior suggested at Çatalhöyük and most certainly in ancient Egypt.

Heracles of Greek mythology (Hercules in the Roman) was given twelve tasks to perform because he got wasted and killed his wife. One of the tasks was to clear the Nemean lion from the grove of Zeus. After killing the beast, he took to wearing the lion's skin with his head sticking out of the lion's mouth. The power comes in because the Nemean lion's skin was impenetrable. This sounds like a play on Lion-man, Cat-men, and Sekhmet discussed earlier.

A Japanese story connected to unusual power of cats is about a geisha named Usugumo as relayed in Davisson (2021, 123):

It so happened that one night, Usugumo's favorite cat began pulling and clawing at her kimono as she entered her bathroom. The cat would not stop, and, of course, Usugumo didn't want her nicest kimono ruined, so she cried for help and a maintenance person responded and cut off the cat's head. The cat's head rolled across the floor and into the bath area where it latched onto and killed a snake coiled in a dark corner. Usugumo then realized the cat was trying to protect her, so she had a statue made of the cat with a raised paw, the maneki-neko.

The cat is so powerful that even in death it can use that power to protect, just as some might call upon the dead, crucified Jesus to help in a crisis. Snakes or serpents can have both a good and an evil side. The uraeus in ancient Egypt, for example, is an upright cobra, symbolizing protection and divine authority. But the cobra had a bad side, and cats were known to dispatch black spitting cobras, indigenous to Egypt, thus representing a powerful, protective force.*

But sometimes being powerful isn't enough, as amply stated by La Fontaine (1983, 70):

> *"Go, paltry insect, nature's meanest brat!"*
> *Thus said the royal lion to the gnat.*
> *The gnat declared immediate war.*

La Fontaine, probably, from his own feelings of powerlessness, pits the lion against a gnat. The gnat taunts the lion into battle where the lion wears himself out trying to swat the gnat who mercilessly bites the lion over and over again. The message here is simple: big people (lions) don't always do well when up against little people (gnats); big does not always lead to victory.

> *For, though so fierce and stout,*
> *By effort wearied out,*
> *He fainted, fell, gave up the quarrel;*
> *The gnat retires with verdant laurel.*

Another connection between cats and snakes is they both hiss. Both the cat and the snake use this sound to signal danger, a warning not given to prey. The snake, similar to the cat, doesn't warn the

---

*Actually, the mongoose is better at dealing with cobras, although it is not immune to the venom as commonly thought.

mouse. So why the warning? The best answer I have is that in battle, even the victor can be seriously injured. The intent of the hiss is to avoid confrontation and allow the other to go on its way. This sounds a lot like peaceful coexistence, a spiritual ideal, but the cat is unlikely to leave the snake alone. The cat is a carnivore and snakes represent food. Also, at least for the species *Felis,* the pupils contract to slits in bright light situations, similar to that of the snake. Lions and tigers, however, have round pupils like ours.

GATE GUARDIANS

Cats have a range of hearing designed to detect the sounds and movements of mice, rats, and other small prey. This range of hearing is around 45–64,000 Hz. This is one of the broadest hearing ranges in the animal kingdom. Cats chose this high frequency hearing without sacrificing low frequency hearing (Heffner and Heffner 1985). Compare this ability to humans who can hear sounds from 64–23,000 Hz. Most humans cannot hear the sounds made by a mouse (around 50,000 Hz), but the cat's ability goes beyond listening for mice and other rodents and extends to hearing, for example, people or predators at a distance, acting as an early warning system. We have catios on both the east and west sides of the house and a large window facing south, and when strange animals or people enter the yard they are tracked from the front of the house to the back—very rapidly. Our ancestors would have noticed a cat's ability to warn of intruders in temples, for example, or that they could detect mice, scorpions, or snakes (like the black spitting cobra) in the fields—a definite asset for farmers (Germond 2001, 77).

Along with the ability to see in the dark and their acute hearing, the cat's tendency to seek out secluded, dark, protected places to hide and sleep connects the cat to role of guardian of the Underworld. Our cats will often sit or recline in a doorway, like a miniature sphinx, probably to detect the comings and goings of the other cats (especially via the cat doors), but sometimes to ambush. The way they position themselves, however, gives the impression that they are guarding those inside. In any case, an early warning system has great survival value.

Cats can also be guardians of specific earthly territories. For example, Warrior-Net (*Wuluo*) has " . . . a human face, with leopard markings, a small waist, white teeth, and he wears earrings" (Strassberg 2002, 146). This strange human-feline guards a particular geography, that is, Green Waist Mountain in China (Nalatizhen, Xinyuan, Ili, Xinjiang, China). Wuluo makes sounds like tinkling jade and also, strangely enough, is connected to fertility, especially for pregnant female visitors wishing to have daughters. The Warrior-Net is comparable to Sekhmet as a guardian, but acts in a similar fertility fashion as Bastet, but limited to a specific territory. As a generalization, Sekhmet is a lion-goddess but Bastet is a cat-goddess, in the sense of the genus *Felis,* with Bastet becoming more popular as the threat of lions diminished. By the New Kingdom (1570–1069 BCE) the cat (likely *Felis catus*) was more available as a mythic theme, one incorporating the cat's bonding and more nurturing nature toward humans.

A famous example of cats and guardians, or so the story goes, is that of the magician and lion and tiger act of Siegfried and Roy. The duo were star performers in Las Vegas from 1990 through 2003 when his white tiger, Mantacore, latched onto Roy Horn's neck and dragged him offstage. There are several stories as to why the cat behaved the way he did. The first is mishandling of the cat by Horn. The other story, which I like better, is that Mantacore was protecting Horn. We will never know for sure. Our cats are certainly protective and act as our guardians, if I read their behavior correctly, by going in front of us as we walk down the hallway, patiently guarding the bathroom entrance like the Sphinx on the Giza Plateau until we finish or waiting at the sliding glass door of my study for my return.

FERTILITY

Bastet, the more recent rendering of the cat-goddess, represents fertility. Her head (sometimes the whole body) is not that of a lion but that of *Felis catus* or perhaps *Felis chaus* (jungle cat), or even *Felis silvestris lybica*. The connection to fertility is quite obvious in that *Felis* is a prolific breeder, having anywhere from two to eight kittens in a litter with possibly five litters per year. But, again, the cat proper is not being worshipped in the case of Bastet; it is the characteristic of fertility. Moreover, mother cats are very protective of their young. Bastet is likewise a protector as revealed in the Coffin Texts of the Middle Kingdom (2030–1650 BCE). These were the so-called Book of the Dead painted on coffins rather than carved into tomb walls of the Old Kingdom (2649–2130 BCE) or written on papyrus in the New Kingdom (1570–1069). Fertility also represents life or bringer of life and this added to the cat's characteristics. This brings into question whether or not the Egyptians prevented individuals from removing cats from Egypt because they thought they were so valuable symbolically and as mousers. It is possible they paid lip service to this, but the reality is that cats breed so rapidly that there is no way this could be prevented. Once several cats made their way onto ships, often loaded with rats and mice, they would quickly multiply, and stealing cats from Egypt became unnecessary. In fact, it is very likely that the Egyptians sold or gave cats to foreigners with whom they traded.

Cats, however, were highly valued by some cultures, for example Japan, but their value was wrapped into the fact that they were rare and only the wealthy could own them. Regardless, in time feline fecundity would alter that value, making the cat available to almost anyone.

NIGHT VISION

Cats have night vision, but this does not mean they can see in total darkness. The density of rods located in the retina at the back portion of the eye is almost three times that of humans. Rods are the most sensitive of the visual receptors and useful at night; there is no way random mutations would have fine-tuned this increase in rods as, in all probability, this increase was gradual and likely occurred long before cats, as we recognize them, were on the landscape. Cats, however, have fewer cones than humans, and cones are more useful during daylight hours (Bradshaw et al. 2012, 27).

Cats are night predators (and daytime opportunists) and they do not need color differentiation to hunt prey. In the back of the retina there is what is called the *tapetum lucidum.* This is a reflective layer that projects light photons outward, allowing the visual pigments to catch photons missed the first time around. This is why the cat's eyes (and those of other animals like dogs, wolves, and horses) glow in the dark; what you are seeing are photons being reflected outward. There are two traits, both genetically inspired, that the ancients saw as spiritual, which are the ability to see in very low light conditions and the glow of the eyes. I see that glow from the eyes on dark nights when I make the rounds, checking waterers and so on—those glowing orbs, when I shine my flashlight, are suspended in space and following my every move. They will even ambush me at the ends of paths, putting out a paw to touch my leg as if counting coup. These traits, I might add, were not necessarily seen as positive and otherworldly at first, but demonic—shades of those demonic predators of a past age. Even today, this characteristic is used to suggest the evil, eerie world of the unknown and of danger. Wolves also possess "night vision" and are often connected to the negative side or the Otherworld. Wolves are greatly feared in Europe, even to this day, I might add, as expressed in folklore and myth. I'm sure that wolves are responsible for some human deaths, but research carried out by Farley Mowat (1963) indicated that at least the Canadian wolves he studied were, like domestic cats, mousers as well as consumers of other small animals. But they were opportunists, and injured deer or humans would be fair game.

STEALTH, CUNNING, AND WISDOM

Cats can move silently from place to place and can appear unexpectedly and disappear without notice. The cat is aided in this by hair that grows off the bottom of its feet, cushioning the cat during movement. This hair also senses vibration on the ground indicating the movement of prey.

The coloring of some cats' fur aids in their stealth. Sid is our Norwegian Forest Cat, with long, disheveled, white and gray fur. In a territory studded with gray rocks and white snow he would be invisible, lying there in perfect stillness, waiting for that rabbit to get just a little closer. Sid is an unusual cat. He wants to be around Katie and me, does not like to be touched, tolerates the other cats, and rarely talks, but he does get playful with us on occasion—but not with the other cats. He is also our major escape artist, and we have taken extreme measures to keep him inside, for he is surely an outside cat. He is strongly bonded with Katie. We acquired Sid when he was only a couple of weeks old and for many weeks bottle fed him in our arms; we talked to him and provided food, warmth, and affection. We can see in Sid shades of the wild cat, a loner domesticated only in recent times; he is very different from the other cats.

But stealth also implies cleverness, because being stealthy requires knowledge and ability to use it in pursuit of prey—or, in the case of La Fontaine's (1983) "The Cat and the Fox," to *avoid being* the prey. In this tale, the cat and fox brag rather noisily about their clever tricks when they approach a group of men and dogs. The cat climbed a tree, safe from the dogs. The fox, however, didn't possess the "trick" of climbing trees and thus "He met two dogs" that did him in. The moral of the story is you might not be as cleaver as you think.

Then there is the story from Russia of "Baba Yaga and the Brave Youth."

Once upon a time . . . this is, in some narrations, a morality story, about a young man living in the woods (representing danger, mystery) with a cat and a sparrow (who represent the wisdom of the ancestors). The youth is warned about a woman who will come to the door and push herself into the room. All will be fine as long as the youth keeps his mouth shut and does not talk to her. Of course, you can't have a good story without danger, so, as you can guess, he can't resist and talks to Baba Yaga, so he is carried off to her house—surrounded by a fence of human bones—down the way.

Reaching the house, Baba Yaga opened the door and threw the brave youth onto the kitchen floor, telling her two daughters to "Cook him up. I'll be back. I have business to attend to!"

Well, one of the daughters insisted that she continue folding clothes while the other took out a big roasting pan from under the sink and, with a loud voice, demanded the youth get in, "So I can cook you up as mother demanded! She will be back in a short time and will be upset if her dinner isn't ready!"

The youth stood up in the pan, and when the daughter tried to put him in the stove, he wouldn't fit. "You're going to have to crouch down or something . . ."

"But, you see," said the youth, "I've never done this before. You will have to show me how."

"Okay, get out of the pan."

The youth got out, and the daughter got in and crouched down, and at that moment he pushed the pan into the oven and cooked the daughter.

The other daughter, hearing the commotion, came into the

kitchen and in shock said, "What have you done? You've cooked my sister. Mother will not be happy at all!"

So, she rolled her sister out of the pan and motioned for the youth to get in, but when she tried to get him into the oven, he wouldn't fit. "You're going to have to crouch down or something . . ."

Finally, Baba Yaga returned to find her two daughters, lying on the kitchen floor, cooked. With great fury she said, "I guess if you want something done right, you have to do it yourself. Now get in the pan, and no funny business!" But, like the daughters before, he wouldn't fit in the oven. "I've never done this before. You'll have to show me how."

And with that, Baba Yaga got into the pan, crouched down, and three's the charm: the youth pushed her into the oven.

There are many variations of this Russian story told to me by my Aunt Jesse many years ago. (I recognized at a young age that the story was similar to Hansel and Gretel.) My aunt was a grade-school teacher and I suspect that she told the toned-down, more politically correct fairytales to her students but told me the originals; perhaps Auntie was trying to tell me something. I especially liked that Cinderella's stepsisters had their eyes pecked out by crows; I guess I figured they deserved it. I am partial to crows as I have a crow spirit as a guardian acquired during a ceremony conducted by an Ojibwe shaman many years ago. This crow spirit is part of my tattooing as the three-legged crow that brings the sun to the top of the Celestial Tree (the axis mundi) in Chinese mythology. This is similar to Re's night journey through the Underworld, emerging as the newborn sun through Nut's vagina in the morning.

Anyway, what is the meaning of the story "Baba Yaga and the Brave Youth"? In Europe the individual is important, along with individual incentive and knowing what to do without being told. This is the exact opposite to the way it is in the Middle East, where you are told what to do by someone in perceived authority, and you had better do it. Why the difference? In the European geography, hunter-gathering behavior requires individual bravery, individual honor, and proving oneself to others—not everyone can kill a deer or a dangerous boar that can end up hunting you. (Remember what happened to the king in *Game of Thrones*?) In the Middle East, we have agricultural communities that predate agriculture in Europe by many thousands of years. Anyone can plow a field or pick a fig; thus, the importance of the individual is minimized. Judaism, Christianity, and Islam emerged from agrarian communities, and in these monotheistic traditions the individual takes second place to God *and* rulers.

The moral of the story of "Baba Yaga and the Brave Youth" is simple: The elders represent wisdom—and they acquired wisdom through living (metaphorically, the bridges they crossed and mountains they climbed). If you aren't going to listen to the elders, then you best be smart enough to get yourself out of the trouble you encounter or create. The cat in this case was seen as wisdom.

Baba Yaga was originally a healing goddess of the Underworld. As an Underworld healing goddess with a knowledge of herbs, for instance, she is likewise connected to mind-altering substances and the rites or rituals connected to their use. With the aid of the Catholic Church she became a demoness who craves human flesh, especially little children. (Perhaps this was society's way of explaining sudden infant death syndrome.) Her behavior is an appeal to the fear of dying and horror of being eaten (cannibalism). And where do you think this originated? You only have to look to the predators, the cats of millions of years ago who killed and ate our relatives on a daily basis. I have been told that a human is the only animal that contemplates its own death. I wonder if this is true.

BRINGERS OF GOOD LUCK

Some cats do not promote evil at all. The yōkai in Japan, for example, is not always evil. The lucky cat yōkai is called maneki-neko (or zhāocái māo in China). In Japan as well as China this is the waving cat mentioned earlier. It dates back to the seventeenth century and is especially suited for luck in business or gambling. On our extended stay in China we encountered zhāocái māo everywhere, especially in taxies and restaurants. We utilized cabs while in Beijing and each had its set of zhāocái māo—there was always more than one. During our stay, we visited several of the indigenous hill tribes in southern China; this was in late December during the rainy season. On one of our adventures we hired a driver to take us into the hills, and when we entered the bus it was difficult not to see all the zhāocái māo lining the dashboard; there were eight of them—a lucky number in China. I wondered why there were so many. Well, we quickly found out. But let me back up.

While in Beijing we took cabs to various temple sites, the Great Wall, and so on. We had heard that Westerners were not allowed to drive in China (at least at that time), and once in the first cab we found out why. Driving in the West is a complex issue when it comes to rules of the road; you know, like you stay on your side, I'll stay on mine, and don't pass on the right. The best way I can describe driving, at least in Beijing, is that it's intuitive or holistic. In other words, find a spot and move ahead to a destination. Spots show up on the right and left, and so we zigged and zagged our way to each destination. One cab driver in particular had three large zhāocái māo on his dash, and, as the cab is much smaller than in the States (at least until recently), bodies are crammed together and it is difficult to miss zhāocái māo swaying back and forth, waving at us, as the driver located and navigated to his next spot.

But back to the bus driver. We knew what to expect in the city, taking cabs and a bus or two day after day, and we thought things might be a little different in the south, west of the Lee River, with more or less wide-open spaces. But no. In Beijing, traffic does not move fast enough, in most cases, and what you encounter are a few fender benders but rarely death. This bus driver was a maniac behind the wheel; I recall my life flashing before my eyes just a few minutes into the trip. We were traveling on narrow, weather-beaten roads, and because of the rain, boulders were rolling down into the road. The bus was slipping and sliding as the driver maneuvered around and over rocks, coming very close to the left side of the highway, which had a vertical drop-off of perhaps fifty or seventy feet! There were no seatbelts, and Katie and I slid back and forth on the bench seat, like the zhāocái māo on the dash, firmly holding onto the bar on the back of the seat in front of us. Then it dawned on me that the driver took his beliefs very, very seriously and fully believed the zhāocái māo would protect him. We did make it to our destination and home again, so perhaps having lots of zhāocái māo will protect as well as bring luck.

As a postscript, as terrifying as the ride was, it was well worth it as we met with some wonderful people—stories I may write about some day. These are hill people, with all the beautiful terracing you see in photos and drawings, and they walk up and down those hills, day after day, and I'm talking *hills*. My wife and I walked up to one village and were greeted by a number of the villagers who showed us their houses, offered us tea, and so on. When it was time to leave my wife took one look back on the path from the village, and said, "I can't walk back down. How in the world did . . ." and with that, one of the elder women who greeted us walked over to my wife, gently locked elbows with her, and walked her down the hill. I might add, it was lightly misting at the time and the rocks on the path were quite slippery. My wife was shocked at the strength of this four-foot, six-inch woman. (Katie is about five-foot, six inches.) I let them go in front of me a few steps before I started down, giving me an opportunity to really appreciate the view of the hillsides from this perspective. I was not in possession of a zhāocái māo at the time; perhaps something rubbed off on the bus ride, and maybe I should stock up. Knowing about cats and what we call superstitions, our bus driver must have strongly believed he was protected from harm, as it is unlikely he drove that way in an attempt to impress us.

The Chinese people love to gamble (and zhāocái māo are certainly useful), and they apparently do not see losing as bad. In fact, it helps redistribute money, and what goes around comes around. We encountered a number of interesting superstitions in China. For example, it is bad luck to leave chopsticks standing up in a bowl. I didn't get a clear statement as to why it was bad luck. We were corrected several times by one of our guides, George, who would reach over and place the sticks horizontally across the bowl. We heard that it is bad luck because it reminds them of incense stuck in bowls at funerals. The number four is unlucky and, like the thirteenth floor in the United States, the hotels we stayed at did not have a fourth floor. The reason given for this avoidance is the word for four is *si* and the word for death is *sei*—they sound the same. Words and symbols have power, with the ultimate form of bad luck being death.

All temples and some houses have a screen or barrier in the entrance-way so you have to walk around it when entering the building. The belief is that evil spirits can only travel in straight lines and having such a barrier prevents them from entering a home. Having a threshold to step over also inhibits evil spirits from entering a home or temple, and it forces the individual to bow. It is best to look down when you step over lest your foot touch the threshold, which can bring more bad luck.

CAT TALK, PURRING, AND CHANTING

Cats talk to humans with whom they have bonded; cat-to-cat talk is very different and quite limited—outside of possible telepathic powers, that is. *Felis catus* seems to be the most talkative of all the *Felis* species (Tavernier et al. 2020) and this is likely by choice and connected to the cat's relationship with humans; attaching themselves to humans was a gamble, a choice that paid off. They had to trust us, and a way of gaining that trust is through talk, by imitating us.

Felis catus can make a variety of sounds, but one thing they cannot do is roar like a lion. The reason for this has to do with the position and nature of the hyoid bone (your Adam's apple), which, for the house cat, resides right under the skull; it is ossified, bonelike, and inflexible. For the lion, it sits further back in the throat, is not ossified, and the vibrations lead to the distinctive roar of the lion.

According to researchers, *Felis catus* has a more sophisticated, more complex vocal inventory than any other member of the cat family, even more so than that of its closest cousin, *Felis silvestris lybica,* the African wildcat. According to Tavernier et al. (2020), this is counterintuitive in that making a lot of noise in the wild would attract predators, but it makes sense when interacting with humans. Our outside cats don't talk much except for sounds made at feeding times and greeting sounds from a couple of the older cats. Think about this. The cat has to realize a difference between being "in the wild" and with humans; they surely understand the difference in communication required for survival in *each* environment. In other words, to live with humans a cat has to behave in some important respects like a human; one of those respects is talking. Not all cats talk to the same degree or variability, and some house cats rarely say anything at all. Currently the most vocal of our cats is Spike, the Maine Coon, and the least is Sid. Spike needs to know where I am and whines and cries until I talk back to him, pet him, or let him in the study (I believe he suffers from separation anxiety). I no doubt have encouraged this behavior. But I talk to *all* the cats, and some respond more than others. So there are obvious personality differences.

Vocalizations include purring, chirping, chirping and chattering, trilling, growling, snarling, hissing, spitting, howling, moaning, wailing, and yowling. I want to add to this snorting and grumbling (part growl and part mumble). There are numerous books and articles online that offer some specifics.*

There are some basic physiological issues that help us to understand why cats and other animals cannot make the sounds available to the human animal. First, a cat does not have mobile lips, and lips are necessary for making certain sounds like "m," "b," and "p." In other words, a cat can't say "meow," contrary to what cat owners hear. The best they can do is, "yeow." Even the ancient Egyptians made this mistake, as their word for cat is "mau." We don't know exactly how to pronounce most ancient Egyptian words because they did not use vowels. But the word cat was likely pronounced "me-ow."

When the cat breathes in and out the change in air pressure causes the folds in the larynx to vibrate, resulting in the purr. For us, these vibrations are part of our speech mechanism (Temple Health 2018).

Purring would have been noticed by the ancients and possibly interpreted as a form of meditation, perhaps a mantra or sound to focus on in order to stop the mind stuff, as found in Buddhism and Hinduism. My experience with cats is that purring usually occurs when in the presence of humans while being pet or brushed or while curled up in one's lap. This is easily interpreted as love or affection—spiritual characteristics. There are a number of animals that make the purring sound (rabbits, squirrels, ring-tailed lemurs, and gorillas, for instance) but the cat will, unlike the gorilla, characteristically curl up in your lap and purr. Purring, however, does not always mean the cat is relaxed and expressing love; the cat could also be ill and perhaps purring is a way to reduce stress. Relaxation is important in the healing process.

Cats also "talk" or rather communicate with their eyes. As mentioned earlier, some researchers discovered if you slowly blink your eyes,

---

*Good places to start include Tavernier et al. (2020), Shojai (2021), and an article entitled "The Cat's Meow" at the Humane Society of the United States website.

your cat will maintain its gaze on you and will often slowly blink its eyes as well. When cats stare at other cats this can touch off aggression, but with humans there appears to be a different message—especially when you slowly blink your eyes. The implied message is friendship or that they are not a threat (McNamee 2017, 96–97; Nagelschneider 2013, 14). This real-life talking to humans carries over into the folklore wherein most of the cats can talk, as do the dogs, mice, and so on.

STARING

But there is a more curious aspect of cat behavior, which obviously gained the attention of the ancient Egyptians and others. Cats, for some strange reason, will stare into space, apparently looking at something we can't see. Perhaps it is a spider on the wall, a bug in the air, or a piece of dust. But there are a couple of other possibilities. One possibility is they are actually seeing things—not dust, a spider, and such, but things our nervous systems cannot detect. Perhaps they see something popping into our dimension, maybe apparitions or other energy forms. Another interpretation, and I suspect considered by the ancients as well, is that the cat goes to another "place," just as the temple priests would when meditating or daydreaming. This would be considered spiritual behavior if not shamanic.

House cats will stare at human caretakers but avert their eyes if we do not blink as mentioned above. We (human caretakers, temple priests) often interpret this behavior as a show of affection or at the very least interest. Or perhaps they access an ancient urge, a hunger for animal flesh; we are, of course, still their food, although an indirect source.

The other consideration is how cats position themselves in doorways as if keeping watch, guarding, crouched down in the manner of the Sphinx on the Giza Plateau. When I am in the bathroom, especially in the morning when the cats are still active, Spike or one of the gingers will position himself in the doorway and will literally, with a paw, prevent another cat from entering—at least for a moment or two. But, as long as I'm in the bathroom and no other cats are around, Spike, for example, will silently stare into the hallway. They seem to go into a trance; trance states are not peculiar to humans. A trance state is an altered form of awareness, a focusing on a sound, image, or physical sensation. Trance is a powerful ability especially for healing as it "stills the brain," reducing stress. I don't know what if anything the cat is experiencing, but the behavior certainly reduces stress as evidenced particularly by the cat's body language.

TRACKING THE VISIBLE AND INVISIBLE

Staring leads us to another interesting characteristic of cat behavior or ability and that is they can see and track flying insects; we can see flies, but we have difficulty tracking them. When a fly, mosquito, or other small insect enters the home living area, our cats will go out of their way to catch it. Cats are not usually very good as pack hunters because, unlike dogs or humans, they get in each other's way. I have seen Nate, the smaller of the three gingers, swat flies out of the air but not actually kill the fly. Another of the gingers, Sherbet, will spend a great deal of time tracking a very small gnat, although I don't know if these two ever catch and kill the insects. The amazing thing is their ability to see and follow these insects in flight. There is not much nourishment in a gnat or fly so it appears these little critters trigger the cat's hunting and stalking instincts. This behavior is separate from simply staring into space, and the two behaviors serve different purposes. Tracking birds and knocking them down in flight is something a cat is well capable of. Their tracking ability seems to match their reflexes, useful in the food quest. Their staring behavior and tracking behaviors, at least in part, are designed for survival, the detection of the slightest movement, and chasing an animal. Moreover, as mentioned above, staring is just one of the many ways a cat reduces stress.

ACROBATIC ABILITIES

Cats are wonderful acrobats—a talent quite necessary when hunting in trees—and one of their sensing features (inner ear) allows them to right themselves within microseconds if they fall. The cat, as long as it is conscious, will land on its feet—usually (Page 2008, 113–14). If dropped from a height of about thirty feet or over, the cat may not recover. This informs us that hunting in trees is dangerous and falls will happen, so the cat maintained or created a number of mechanisms for survival in that environment. The ancient Egyptians and others must have seen this as magical. This ability develops early (Bradshaw, Casey, and Brown 2012). Any behavior distinct from that of the human animal is likely to have been seen as otherworldly by our ancestors.

MAINTENANCE OF JUVENILE CHARACTERISTICS

As Bradshaw, Casey, and Brown comment (2012, 8):

> In behavioral terms, domestication has probably had less effect on the cat than on any other domestic animal. The changes that have taken place seem to be of three kinds: (i) reduction in brain size, often correlated in other domesticated animals with a reduced sensitivity to uncongenial stimuli; (ii) modification of the hormone balance, mainly by reduction in the size of the adrenals; and (iii) neoteny, the persistence of some juvenile behavior characteristics in the adult.

In terms of predatory behavior seen in kittens, this continues into adulthood. In other words, it isn't lost or toned down as it is in dogs. According to Bradshaw, Casey, and Brown (2012, 9), for dogs the predatory behavior is "incomplete." In this respect, cats seem to "stay young," and this ability might have been seen as otherworldly. Keep in mind that each cat is an individual, and different cats have different behavioral patterns and potentials, just as with humans, and this is to be expected.

SLEEPING

Cats sleep on average twenty hours a day. Being flexible, they will often attune sleep habits to that of their human caretakers. This is where we get the expression "catnap." During the day our indoor cats will sleep an hour or so, arise, and play if another cat is available, but usually they make their presence known by "talking," rubbing against me and, my favorite, stroking me with a paw, often with claws slightly extended. This is a signal that it needs to be pet or sometimes to lead me to its latest captured prey: one of my wife's hair ties. Temple priests would have noticed this behavior as well.

Cats dream, as do most mammals, evidenced by twitching, moving their paws, and mouth movements with muffled vocalizations. They can go into deep delta sleep—as if hibernating. Bears do the same thing, but for many weeks or months, and this is a way of preserving energy when food is not readily available as during the winter months. Cats seem to hibernate for several hours each day, perhaps as a way to save energy, similar to hummingbirds. Dreaming was an important divination procedure in ancient Egypt, where priests were paid to dream (Szpakowska 2003). They must have assumed the cat was doing the same and could access the other world, the world of deities and demons.

Dreams are apparently necessary for proper physiological balance, but dream interpretation, at least for humans, is a personal matter. We share many symbols and images when awake, that is, trees, cars, people, and so on, but what they mean is an individual matter. The world of the cat is very different, and when a cat is dreaming the content is a mystery. However, our ancient ancestors of thirty million years ago at least at times dreamed of cats, and the cats, likewise, dreamed of our ancestors. The point is cats and humans dream and whatever purpose dreams serve for humans it would likely be the same for cats. Again, if the priests used dreams to connect to the spiritual world, they would assume cats could do this as well. More about dreams in chapter 7.

VOMITING

Cats are notorious for vomiting hairballs, although dogs can do this as well. Besides sleeping, cats spend a great deal of time grooming and, in the process, swallow large amounts of hair. Most will pass through the digestive system (some of it is digested). Large amounts of hair are expelled orally and what comes out in the vomit is called a "*trichobezoar*—a damp wad of undigested hair, moistened by bile and other digestive fluids—and commonly referred to as a hairball. Despite that term, hairballs are rarely globular in shape. Rather, they are most often slender and cylindrical" (Cornell, "Hairy Dilemma").One has to wonder how the ancients saw this behavior and the result. The cat gets really close to the ground, retching occurs, and up comes a hairy cylinder that looks like a miniature mummy. This image is sort of like Anubis attending the mummification of Osiris, preparing him for his role as the Judge of the Dead in the Underworld. Nowhere have I encountered references to cats and hairballs, especially in the various medical texts, so this is pure speculation on my part.

CATS AS SHAMANS, TRICKSTERS, AND MONSTERS

Cats, and understandably so for seasoned cat lovers, have a reputation for being "bad." Cats are curious. In order to survive in their world for millions of years they had to know the nature of the territory that will provide the calories necessary for their continued existence. This translates into being curious *and* cautious with new information (a fallen limb, a hole in the ground, or new smells, for instance). As an example, especially in the winter months, we put mats on the floor near entranceways. When we first put them down the cats will often jump back when they see this new "thing" on the ground, then cautiously approach it and perhaps smack the carpet, but at the very least they'll smell it then tag it with a scent from the side of their head. Cats do not see very clearly up close, and they will often use their whiskers when they examine unfamiliar objects.

With that said, our cats will get up on a table and move things around as if searching for something, often times bringing "play" things down to the floor. This appears to be part of their juvenile programming that remains with cats into old age. Their curiosity, their sometimes destructive nature, and our programmed fear of the dark precipitated by ancient predators all translate into mythic themes of monster cats, evil shape-shifters, and demons of all types and sizes. Cats, as Vocelle aptly points out, have been revered and reviled. She comments:

> Aesop (620–546 BC) used the cat as a prominent character in approximately 15 fables. Based on Greek myths, some of the fables such as *The Cat and Venus*, and others in fact borrowed from stories originating in India. The fable has been added to and changed throughout the centuries, and it is certain Aesop did not write all the fables we have today. The cat's character in these stories is predominately one of an intelligent, sly, conniving trickster bent on self-preservation. (2017, 59)

Much of what is attributed to Aesop has a lot to do with consequences which tricksters often unwittingly reveal. The goddess Venus is not often described as a trickster, but you decide. In Aesop's *The Cat and Venus* we encounter a test, to see if personality and behavior can be altered. In short, a cat falls in love with a handsome man and begs Venus to change him into a beautiful maiden, which Venus does immediately. The cat—now a beautiful maiden—and the handsome lad marry, but Venus was curious as to whether or not the changes in body matched changes in behavior.

Thus Venus unleashed a mouse and the maiden took chase. Well, the body had changed but the maiden was still a cat at heart, and thus Venus changed the maiden back into a cat. The moral of the story: the outer self can change but the inner self remains the same (Aesop 1912).

What exactly is a trickster? A trickster is a deceiver but can also be a magical helper with secret knowledge. One of the more famous tricksters known to all is the Cheshire Cat from Lewis Carroll's *Alice's Adventures in Wonderland*. In this case, the cat offers riddles but teaches important lessons. I always considered the Cheshire Cat to be a reflection of Alice communicating with herself while in an altered dream state. For me, this enters the quantum level, the waveform. In this sense, Alice *is* the Cheshire Cat. I will discuss waveforms in chapter 7.

Another famous trickster is Loki, a shape-shifter taking on the forms of a fly, mare, flea, and salmon, but never a cat. He is best known for creating chaos among the gods, but he is helpful as well.

The trickster god in ancient Egypt was Seth, the evil younger brother of Osiris, who killed Osiris through trickery. Seth symbolizes the mystery and evil in the desert but also *social evil*. Apophis or Apepi, the monstrous cosmic serpent of the Underworld, stands for *cosmic evil*, and neither social nor cosmic evil can be eliminated, for to do so would remove any reference to good and collapse the paired opposites that scientists claim make up the tangible universe. The following story is called the "Osiris Round," and understanding the symbols in this story allows a general overview of Egyptian metaphysics. This, by the way, may be the original Cain and Able story.

Osiris stands for good and fertility, and Seth symbolizes evil and death, the opposite of fertility, while the symbol seventy-two equals precession. This refers to how the zodiac moves one degree of arc approximately every seventy-two years, and by multiplying 72 by 360 you get 25,920 years, the time it takes planet Earth, which has a cyclic wobble, to make one complete rotation of its axis through the celestial sphere.

Although Magi (2009, 274–76) suggests the number seventy-two may mean "absolutely nothing," why does such a strange number show up in Egyptian, East Indian, Chinese, Mayan, and Aztec myths (Santillana and von Dechend 1969)?

Be that as it may, fourteen represents one-half of the phases of the moon, symbolizing life, death, and return (remember the moon "stands still" for approximately one day during its cycle each month). Sekhmet represents the guardian, with serious intent and consequences, while Bastet represents fertility and childbirth. Isis stand for loyalty and purity, while Nephthys represents the sexual goddess of the household—this is the angel in the morning and devil at night in some country-western songs. Also, some of the players change depending on whether an Egyptian, a Greek, or Joseph Campbell is telling the story. As the story goes . . .

One dark night when Isis, the sister and wife of the pharaoh Osiris, was away from the palace, Nephthys, Seth's wife and sister, snuck into Osiris's bedroom and had sex with him. He was dead asleep and did not know the difference, or at least this is what he told Isis, who didn't seem too upset about it. From this union was born the jackal-headed boy, Anubis. Seth was enraged and, because he wanted to be pharaoh, he decided to murder his brother.

So one dark night Seth snuck into Osiris's bedroom and took very accurate measurements of his body. He was able to come away unnoticed because Osiris was dead asleep. Seth gave the measurements to his royal coffin maker: "Make this coffin using these measurements, exactly. And make this the most beautiful coffin ever, like no other in the kingdom."

With these instructions, the coffin maker went to his shop and, using the best Lebanese cedar and his finest tools, carved the most perfect coffin. It took some time to get things exact, but after one month the coffin was ready, just in time for the festival. All were invited, wearing their best apparel, wigs and all, and when the party was in full swing, Seth rolled out this beautiful coffin and offered a challenge: "Come and try the coffin, and anyone it fits perfectly can have it!"

Well, Neith tried, Sekhmet tried, and others; they all climbed in to try it out, but it fit no one perfectly. Finally, after much prompting, Osiris climbed in—it fit perfectly, and with that, seventy-two attendants came out from behind a curtain, slapped on the lid, placed fourteen bronze bands around the coffin to keep the lid secure, and they threw it in the Nile, drowning the unsuspecting Osiris.

He floated down the Nile, into the Delta and ultimately the Mediterranean, and finally, during a storm, the coffin with the dead Osiris inside was thrown way up onto a beach in Lebanon. Time went by, but, of course, time does not exist in myth, and the roots of a Lebanese cedar grew from the coffin, from which a beautiful cedar tree emerged. It gave off a wonderful aroma and so entranced the king in those parts that he ordered the tree cut down, fashioned into a pillar, and brought into the palace and placed in the center of what would be the nursery for a soon-to-be-born prince.

Isis, meanwhile, went in search of her beloved brother and husband, following the Nile and, understanding sea currents, finally entering Lebanon, where she encountered three young maidens at a well. After fixing their hair and acting very motherly toward them, Isis learned that a prince has been born to the king and queen down the way and they require a nursemaid. Isis knew that Osiris was somewhere in the palace; after all she is a goddess. She thanked the young ladies and off she went to the palace, where she was welcomed and straight away given the job as nursemaid.

Once in the nursery she could feel Osiris's presence in the pillar in the palace of the powerful king. She needed to bring Osiris back to Egypt, for no Egyptian ever wanted to be buried in a foreign land, but for the moment she had a prince to attend to. During the day she fed the prince through her little finger, giving him power, strength, and knowledge, and at night she placed him in the fireplace to burn off his mortal self and make him immortal—the least she could do to thank the king and queen for their hospitality. And while he was in the fireplace, Isis would morph into a swallow and mournfully fly round and round the pillar.

This went on for many nights until one night the king and queen unexpectedly came into the nursery and saw this bird twittering around the pillar and their child burning up in the fireplace! The queen, as you can imagine, let out a scream and broke the spell, and the child died in the flames.

With that, Isis morphed back into herself, brought the child back to life, explained the situation regarding Osiris and his current residence in the pillar, and asked permission to take Osiris home. Permission was granted. The pillar was placed on a barge and Isis and the dead Osiris headed back to the Delta. Once deep in the Delta, Isis removed the coffin from the pillar, removed the bronze bands and lid, and laid closely upon the dead Osiris, conceiving Horus. Some time went by and, aided by lion-headed Sekhmet as protector and Bastet, the goddess of childbirth, Isis brought Horus, the God of Light, into the world through virgin birth.

Shortly thereafter, Seth was chasing a boar in the swamp and came upon the body of Osiris. In a rage he tore Osiris into fourteen pieces and scattered them around the landscape. Now Isis had to search for Osiris all over again and, with the help of Anubis, located thirteen of the fourteen pieces. The fourteenth piece fell into the Nile and was consumed by a fish—the origin of the fish meal on Friday in the Catholic tradition, the consumption of the sacred flesh. Meanwhile, Anubis reassembled Osiris and prepared him for his trip into the Underworld, where he went from being a fertility god in the Upper World to being Judge of the Dead in the Underworld.

What does this have to do with cats? Well, Sekhmet was at the party and at the birthing of Horus as protector, and Bastet represents fertility—both are major characteristics attributed to cats. Tricksters and evil demons are always afoot (pregnant women were considered magnets for demons because of high rates of infant mortality), and a trickster cannot exist without a protector. We see then, in mythic themes, some basic characteristics of cats as guardians and agents of fertility. Both attributes would have been appreciated as spiritual because of what they guard: the son of the goddess Isis and the god Osiris— Horus, the God of Light and fertility—representing the bringing forth of new life in the round of life, death, and return.

The ultimate trickster cat in European folklore is Puss in Boots, with the oldest telling of the story attributed to Italian author Giovanni Straparola around 1550 CE, but usually Charles Perrault (1628– 1703 CE) is given the credit. In the story, Puss in Boots, like many tricksters, uses his intelligence to gain wealth and power and finally marries a princess.

The Japanese lore contains a fascinating list of monsters called yōkai as mentioned earlier (Foster 2015; Nishimoto 2021). Perhaps some of these monsters are or were real—animals encountered in the woods—or perhaps they were shadows on the wall or some sort of drug-related hallucination or otherwise. Many of these would come under the category of urban legends, or in other cases, rural legends, and some of the monsters were real cats. A number of these cats called *kaibyō* ("strange cats") are depicted as just plain evil. In the following there is some repetition of Japanese and Chinese material in order to make different points.

In Japan cats are believed to be cursed and to possess witchcraft. They are malevolent spirits. Spectral cats can grow to gigantic size and terrorize whole villages, even though they are barely visible. Their gigantic faces and menacing grins may haunt people as they slowly become visible through a wall, then fade away again.

It is also said that cats have power over the dead and the demons, especially the sea spirits. Japanese sailors believed that the souls of the drowned never found peace, so they kept a cat on their ship to protect them against the invasion of sea spirits, the sad souls of the thousands of drowned sailors who went to rest in the earth (Knappert 1992, 41–42).

Cats, you see, have both a good and bad side, and each needs a story, a warning of sorts.

And being strange creatures, they are strangers, and strangers are capable of doing bad things. Davisson (2021, 53) comments: "Beware of keeping your sweet and loving house cat for too long. Once that venerable kitty reaches sufficient age, its tail will split into two and it will begin to walk on its hind legs. Possessed of fierce powers, your cat will begin its second life as a nekomata, a terrifying breed of yōkai."

As you have probably noticed, when talking about Japanese yōkai—of the cat variety or any other—you will usually hear about them in conjunction with the Edo period (1603–1867 CE). Not only was this the golden age of the arts, but it was also the golden age of yōkai. Most of Japan's monsters were born at this time. But nekomata debuted five centuries prior to other breeds of supernatural cats. Their roots run deep.

Nekomata have the powers of necromancy—raising and controlling the dead, turning the dead into something resembling zombies. They are also connected to unusual experiences or events as a way of explaining a mysterious fire or accident.

What I find most interesting about Davisson's statement above is the emergence of most of the monsters in Japanese folklore during a specific time span—when there is a rather fluid society and one might be surrounded by strangers. Fear of strangers can be traced back to—you guessed it—the strangers, the cats who were eating our ancestors as, initially, our only relationship was their hunger and us as food. Strangers can "eat you alive" or otherwise make your life miserable.

Cats also have the reputation of being blood-sucking vampires called *bakeneko*. In Japan it is related that Prince Hizen once had a mistress who was in reality either a giant cat or had a feline spirit. Every night she put a spell on the guards and entered the prince's bedroom. Gradually the prince fell ill, his condition deteriorated, and soon it became clear that he was dying. At last a soldier by the name of Ito Soda was found prepared to keep watch. He turned a dagger in his flesh so that the pain kept him awake, and so he did not fall asleep in spite of the cat-demon witchcraft. The mere sight of his watchful eyes in the dark made the demoness powerless. She stayed away and after a few nights the prince recovered (Knappert 1992, 316).

But there are other categories of yōkai one of which is *kasha*. Davisson (2021, 67) comments: "Kasha are one of the biggest conundrums amongst Japan's yōkai. Over the centuries, kasha have evolved from a fiery cart pulled by devils to an aged cat that changes into a corpse-eating monster. Even calling them yōkai is on the dubious side. They have more in common with religious figures like the brutal, hell-dwelling oni who mete out punishment in the Buddhist afterlife. Although yōkai can be a catch-all term for monsters, kasha are more properly demons."

Perhaps their demonic nature accounts for the fact that while other kaibyō like nekomata and bakeneko have become huggable cartoons in modern times, kasha remain fearsome creatures. There is nothing even remotely cute about kasha.

The stories regarding corpse-eating cats may have some validity to it. U.S. soldiers who served in Vietnam report seeing tigers or leopards responding to firefights and dragging off the dead and wounded and even attacking the living on night patrols (there are numerous stories on the internet). Combat and the noise produced through gunfire, swords clashing, and certainly the moans and groans of the wounded and dying would most certainly attract the attention of scavengers and predators. Cat are curious and opportunists and would definitely drag off fresh kill caused in any manner.

Shuker (2020, 101–2) cites a report from 1969 of U.S. troops near the Cambodia border spotting a tiger described as follows: "The tiger was white where a tiger is white and black where a tiger is black, but all the orange parts were a pale green." The soldiers were awestruck, as if hallucinating. The animal did not seem the least afraid of the men and eventually, after minutes of a stare down, the tiger leisurely walked away. Shuker's work (*Mystery Cats of the World Revisited*) makes the point that strange animals, in this case cats, are to be found in many unexpected places, and it is quite possible that, although embellished, many sightings of unusual, out-of-context animals, perceived as angels and demons, still occur throughout the world.

The kasha, or demon cat, is connected to Shintoism, the early shamanic tradition of Japan, likely related to the Bonpo shamanic tradition existing in Asia long before the advent of Buddhism. Kasha is considered, as mentioned, a yōkai, or supernatural monster, spirit, or demon in Japanese folklore. But they can also act as judges in the underworld, often snatching away bodies at funerals.

Shintoism, again the older shamanic tradition in Japan, defines the house cat as a dangerous supernatural entity generally referred to as yōkai with the bakeneko, kasha, and nekomata as specific types of yōkai. Yōkai come in all sizes, from the size of a rat to that of a human. Some walk on two legs. Some are able to appear and disappear at will, and others employ shape-shifting, taking on the appearance of ordinary cats or humans, including their master, both male and female. They can be tricksters but as mentioned in some stories (e.g., those about kasha) they are more sinister: they eat their masters or worse, steal corpses from graveyards and eat them. The reference is to the kasha as trickster, sometimes a cannibal, sometimes a demon—kasha can take on many demonic personalities.

Foster (2015, 215–16) comments further on the bakeneko:

There are numerous examples of yōkai cats in Japanese folklore, where they are portrayed as everything from lighthearted tricksters to vicious monsters. Presumably the quiet, intelligent mien of the cat, along with its stealthy prowling behavior and powerful vocal abilities, contributes to a sense of mystery and otherworldliness. In Japan, like many places in the world, cats seem to occupy an ambiguous position in human lives; they sit calmly, purring, on our laps one minute and go off chasing rats the next. They are both domestic and wild, comfortable in either urban or rural environments, simultaneously an intimate part of the human world and part of the natural world. Perhaps it is not surprising that cats, both feral and domestic, play an important role in yōkai folklore. [...]

Toriyama Sekien illustrates a nekomata in his first catalog; it stands on two legs on the outer veranda of a house, with a small towel (*tenugui*) on its head. Another cat—presumably not a yōkai—sits on the ground below it, while a third seems to be looking out from inside the house. Although Sekien does not explain anything here, the nekomata is portrayed as betwixt and between the human and animal worlds. It is wild but wears a towel on its head, stands on two legs like a person, and is perched literally on the outer edge of a human habitation, with one cat outside (feral?) behind it and another inside (domestic?) in front of it. The fact that there is no commentary suggests that the nekomata was such a commonly recognized yōkai that explanation was not necessary.

Another yōkai cat is called *bakeneko*, which might be loosely translated as "monster cat." [...] The most famous bakeneko narrative is "Nabeshima no bakeneko sodo" (The disturbance of the bakeneko of Nabeshima), a legend the developed from a succession dispute, known as the Nabeshima Disturbance, that occurred in Hizen (present-day Saga Prefecture) in the late 1500s. Some versions of the Nabeshima legend are simple tales of revenge, while others recount a complex plot featuring a demon cat in the guise of a woman who is foiled only by the intense loyalty of one of the Nabeshima clan retainers. The narratives themselves probably did not originate until the late Edo period, long after the original disturbance, but they became popular through sensationalist Kabuki and *kyogen* plays, as well as through wood-block-print illustrations. In the twentieth century, versions of the tale were made into movies, such as *Hiroku Kaibyo-den* (*The Haunted Castle*, 1969, dir. Tanaka Tokuzo).

There is a Japanese tale entitled "The Cat Monster Mansion," (Nishimoto 2021, 273–75) which combines elements of Steven King's *Pet Cemetery* with the Aesop fable "Androcles and the Lion."

There once was a maid in a household who was very kind to the family cat, something lacking in the behavior of the lady of the house. In fact, the lady of the house wished the cat gone from the premises. Well, one day she got her wish and the maid was heartbroken to lose her friend and companion.

One day a priest told her he had seen the cat down the way in a large mansion on a faraway island. The maid asked for time off, which was granted, and off she went in search of the cat. Upon arriving at her destination, she was informed of lodging at a mansion not far away. At the mansion she said she was looking for her beloved cat, which received a strange reply: "Are you looking to be eaten too?" However, she was guided to her room. Eventually she met up with her beloved cat, who gave her a large sum of money and told her to get as far away from this place as quickly as possible.

Relieved her cat was safe, she left her cat behind with great sadness and returned home, money in hand, and told the lady of the house what transpired. The lady of the house, thinking that she had cared for the cat, decided to go to the mansion and likewise receive a reward. This she did, and she was quickly eaten by the cats.

The moral of the story is to be good to monsters and they may return in kind, but it also points out the dual nature of cats, both good and evil.

The Chinese and Japanese share a number of myths with the *Huan,* a cat-like creature found in Chinese mythology, which is similar to the nekomata in Japanese myths. The Huan is described as a medium-sized cat-like creature with a single eye and three tails. Along with this, possessing the Huan's pelt is said to confer luck to its owner, and it also has medicinal qualities. Although not quite the same as the leopard skin in significance, there are some similarities. More about the Huan shortly.

The Chinese have an abundance of monsters in their mythology, most of which are peculiar to specific geographies: hills, valleys, swamps, and so on. Much of the following material was drawn from *Classic of Mountains and Seas,* attributed to a Chinese poet named Tao Yuanming, whose dates are around 365–427 CE, but it is likely a combined effort. One interesting thing about the animals referenced is that some of them may have been real, though embellished, of course. One of these is represented by the guardian lions (also called Fu Dogs) in front of the gates to the Forbidden City in Beijing, China. As you enter past the lions facing you, the one on your right is male (yang), clutching a ball or globe in his right paw, representing the world, the domain of the emperor (male). The female is on your left (yin). She has a baby lion under her left paw. She is the ruler of the house and all that goes on in it. On the head of each there are bumps, and it is my understanding that the more bumps the more powerful the lion and, of course, the king and queen symbolize. Also, both have five fingers or claws, and only the king and queen can have statues of lions guarding the home or lion emblems on clothing, and so on, with five fingers or claws. This shows you the power of symbols and the density of their meanings or references; symbols point in many directions at the same instant. The following, again, are composite animals and are from Jiankun Sun's *Fantastic Creatures of the Mountains and Seas* (2021).

Xiwangmu, a creature considered "Queen Mother of the West," possesses "the upper form of a woman, [...] a leopard's tail, a tiger's fangs behind seductive lips, and the howl of a wild animal. Her tangled hair was held in place by jade ornaments. Charged with arranging calamities, pestilences, and punishments among earthlings, she functioned like an ominous constellation. While not manifestly unattractive, the nontraditional, almost feral beauty of this daunting creature exuded an inauspicious aura, owing to the dreadful events under her charge" (Sun 2021, 62–63).

Here we are into cause and effect, of needing something or someone to blame for bad happenings. Also, we are confronted with the unknown which translates into danger simply because we can't predict what we will encounter in the woods.

The Huan, described earlier, could very well be imaginings grafted to a feral cat, fox, or some other similar animal. Jiankun Sun describes the Huan: "[This] odd creature called the Huan, a one-eyed, three-tailed feline that was said to be a superb mimic. It was reputed by some to have the ability to imitate the calls of a hundred animals. . . . No definitive evidence has ever been found to substantiate claims that this truly remarkable creature possessed the power to ward off demons and evil spirits, and that eating its flesh was a cure for jaundice. No use was found for the tails" (Sun 2021, 70–71).

We theoretically live in a universe of paired opposites (at least), but only when we enter the field of time (the physical world) and in the wilderness are we likely to encounter positive spirits as well as negative, evil spirits.

Bo, a magic horse-like creature that was, according to the narrative, a domesticated creature, is described as follows: "The majestic Bo had a pure white body, a pitch-black tail, and a single horn that pointed skyward from the bridge of its nose. Its teeth and front hooves resembled the fangs and claws of a tiger, though less pronounced. Possessing a drumbeat call, this domesticated creature protected human riders from the terrors of war, partly because it fed not on vegetarian fare, but on tigers and leopards. As it carried its rider through dense woods of Zhongqu shan, even the most powerful predators kept their distance" (Sun 2021, 78–79).

Riding magical beasts speaks to our desire for abilities we cannot possess. With modern technology we can possess some of those abilities but for our ancestors all they had were experiences, imaginations, and narratives. There are flying horses in many traditions—for example, Pegasus of the Greek and Devadatta of the Hindu tradition. Also recall the winged horse (Abraxan) in *Harry Potter*. In the case of the Bo and Abraxan, they are protectors, not just transportation entities.

Humans have the capacity to imagine and many of these imaginings obviously involved the need to combine aspects of numerous known creatures, their powers and abilities. The Zhujian was a bizarre mountain creature, "[with] a face whose features seemed misplaced or underdeveloped, with a single eye above embedded nostrils and a small mouth between bovine ears. Its body was that of a very large leopard, replete with spots, and an extraordinarily long tail it kept off the ground when it walked by holding it in its mouth. The reputedly prehensile tail lay coiled beside the creature's body when it rested" (Sun 2021, 94–97).

The Zhujian is simply bizarre and it is perhaps because the animal was bizarre that it lies "outside," characteristic of the unknown. This is the way we imagine space aliens, the unfamiliar "other."

The Shebishi was likely a real animal, the lion. The name for lion in Chinese is *shi*, which, as the reader can see, is part of Shebishi. Sun describes: "Shebi is the Shelong or Dragon, a creature with the body, tail, and claws of a fierce feline, the face of a human, but with intense eyes, a horn emanating from just above its snout, and enlarged ears from which snakes dangle" (Sun 2021, 248–51).

Although the Shi (lion) does not have a human face it would seem that the Shebishi is likely the model for the Chinese dragons that protect the inhabitants of the Forbidden City. According to the description of the Shebishi: "It is one of the stranger gods in the compilation, and for unknown reasons, it was killed by a superior god. Its spirit, however, was not exterminated and continued to live in the form of a corpse" (Sun 2021, 248–51).

The god-like status given to the Shebishi is another reason for connecting it to the shi. The above description indicates that the spirit of the shi, just as kingship, is immutable, although the body may die, similar to the adage "The king is dead; long live the king."

Most of the creatures described in *The Classic of Mountains and Seas* and illustrated in *Fantastic Creatures of the Mountains and Seas* are directly related to that primal fear our ancient ancestors generated in the face of predators, strangers, and the unknown and mysterious, outsiders all. A leopard is bad enough, but what if there are even worse creatures afoot?

MORE ABOUT THE MONSTER-CAT

Cryptozoology is the study of legendary creatures existing mainly through stories told over time. Because no real tangible evidence exists to scientifically back up their claimed existence, they fall into the category of "cryptozoology." In other words, all things are possible along with the fact that we have encountered fish and other animals thought to be long extinct. Such stories include the Yeti, the Loch Ness Monster, and the Kraken, that enormous sea monster that resides off the coast of Norway. From Northern Europe to China, Southeast Asia, and Africa, and from Canada to the tip of South America there are claims of monstrous beasts, some of which are cats.

The Celts had a long association with cat monsters, but they also strongly identified with the cat's power.

The domesticated feline has long played a role in the Celtic imagination, although not so prominent as that of the dog or of several large wilder animals. Cat features adorning ancient carved heads may imply fearfulness. The cognomen of the Irish usurper Cairbre Cinn-Chait means "cat head." There are several monster cats in Celtic tradition, including the cat sith of the Highlands and the Cath Paluc of

Wales. Aibill was changed into a white cat by Clidna. The Shetlands were known as Inise Cat [Cat Islands] in earlier Scottish Gaelic tradition. The former shire of Caithness was apparently named for an ancient people whose emblem was the cat. In Scotland also, live cats were roasted in a brutal divination rite known as taghirm. In Irish folklore the Kilkenny cats represented a mutually self-destructive enmity in a story that appears to have an origin in political experience. Elsewhere in Irish tradition black cats were thought to be lucky, and the blood of a black cat was thought to cure St. Anthony's fire (erysipelas). (MacKillop 1998, 69)

MacKillop mentions the "cat sìth," about which we know a great deal. I have consulted with relatives in Scotland and it appears many of these stories are no longer told. The following comes from "The World's Creepiest Cat Legends" (2018):

A fairy creature from both Celtic and Scottish mythology, Sith Cats were large black cats with splashes of white fur on their chests. While Sith Cats were believed to be spectral in nature, they were inspired by actual creatures known as Kellas cats, a hybrid between wildcats and domestic cats only found in Scotland. They were believed to have wicked purposes, including a desire to consume souls immediately after death. Every year on Samhain (which we now celebrate as Halloween), houses where an offering of a saucer of milk was left outside would be blessed by the being, while those that did not would suffer a curse. Fun fact: The Scots believed the Cat Sith was actually a witch that had the ability to transform into a cat, but that the witch was limited to only nine transformations in a lifetime. Scholars believe this is the origin of the belief that cats enjoy nine lives!

Although narratives of Irish imaginary creatures were constructed millennia ago, sightings still occur. Legends of haunted houses are abundant in Dublin, one being the Killakee House on Downton Abbey, haunted by a supposed monster cat (Life's Abundance 2018).

Even Iceland has its cat monster tales, some likely originating with the Vikings hundreds of years ago, but not this one—the story of the merciless Jólakötturinn who stalks the countryside looking for anyone not wearing fine new clothes. Apparently this is a more recent story spread by farmers desiring to encourage the completion of wool processing before autumn (Van Huygen 2017). So what we have is an economically inspired monster.

Then there are black cats as referenced in the Gallic stories, and one has to wonder how much influence the Catholic Church had in demonizing cats, especially black cats. "The King of the Cats" is a British tale about a grave digger who encounters nine black cats walking down the road carrying a small coffin with a crown on it. The grave digger is told by one of the cats to "tell Tommy Tildrum that Timmy Toldrum is dead." When retelling the event to his wife, the family cat heard the story and stated, "What? Old Tim dead? Then I'm the King o' the Cats!" That said, the cat ran up the chimney never to be seen again (Van Huygen 2017). This may be an expression of "The King is dead. Long live the king!"

We remember and pass on many of these tales, but what I find interesting is that we hear these stories early in life and then are encouraged to give up most of them as fact, except those that serve other social or mystical purposes. This is much different from what goes on in many other cultures where the early stories are maintained throughout a person's lifetime. Also, mainly in the West, there are stories for children and stories for adults. Many years ago, my next-door neighbor, and more recently my Italian informants, cautioned that pregnant women (magnets for demons in many cultures) should avoid handling cats as they can cause birthmarks on the fetus, a common European story. In England this could be the actual shape of the cat's face, and in Portugal cats can infect the baby with a hairy wart. Some English stories, however, report that black cats given as a wedding gift are lucky, especially if the cat sneezes in the presence of the bride (Van Huygen 2017).

From Burma and other areas of Southeast Asia we hear that cats are keepers of souls. In Laos, for example, souls are souls and they can migrate, and it doesn't make any difference what animal they go into—they become part of that animal's life force. I call this soul-shifting, somewhat like organ transplants. Let's say the soul of your legs leaves you, and you have trouble walking. In Laos, the Hmong shaman (*Txiv Neeb*) can replace it with that of a cow or even a chicken. I heard a story about a Hmong tribesman who was badly wounded in a firefight with Pathet Lao in the 1960s but was dragged away by the Hmong survivors. A shaman administered to his wounds, but he died. According to the shaman, just as his soul left his body, it went into a nearby leopard cat (*Prionailurus bengalensis*) that he had as a pet. As the story goes, this shaman, who fought with U.S. troops to deal with the unspeakable horrors put upon the Hmong by the Pathet Lao, left Laos in 1975, brought the leopard cat to the United States, and to this day it is said the cat haunts the streets in one city enacting revenge on those who hurt or injure Hmong people, especially women, acting as a sort of cat superhero. Soul-shifting is a common belief. When a Hmong shaman sacrifices a chicken in order to bring the chicken's soul to, for example, a sick child, the soul, in this sense is just energy to replace that which is missing. During extreme stress and death, the soul can take on the personality of the deceased and transfer to another animal or person.

For the Hmong, and more broadly, souls are not necessarily evil in themselves, but the legend told above offers insights into the cat's perceived powers for good and evil purposes.

Monster cats are found in many areas of Southeast Asia. For example, in Malaysia they say that hidden in the cat's body there is an evil spirit, *badi.* Therefore a cat must never be permitted to touch the body of a dead person, for the spirit would slip into the corpse and revive it, becoming a horrifying ghost (Knappert 1992, 42).

Buddhists in Japan are not especially fond of cats, but Buddhists in other areas find cats loyal and honorable enough to be containers for human souls. In former times, in Siam and Burma, worthy human souls at death would reside in a cat, and when the cat died the soul would pass on to paradise. This is another example of soul-shifting. In more recent times in Siam, now Thailand, the king, during coronation, is given a cat bedecked with jewels. The belief is that the soul of the old king entered the body of this particular cat and so the old king can now participate in the ceremony (Van Huygen 2017). Again, this seems to be a play on the concept of "The king is dead. Long live the king."

THE AMERICAS—REAL AND IMAGINED CATS

Monsters are embedded in a great deal of the American myths and legends, especially urban legends, and much of this, again, can be attributed to "strangers" among us, first the Europeans, and then, in more recent times, "strangers" from all over the world. Remember, humans are a small-group animal; we are not designed to live in these urban areas, and any stranger is potentially dangerous. Where did this fear come from? Right—cats, prowling in the night on the ground and in the trees, were strangers, and you knew that their presence symbolized danger; this is embedded in our genes.

Then there are more bizarre tales, such as those reported by the Pueblo and Navajo Indians of the southwest United States of cats in the shape of cacti, who, with sharp knives for paws, collect and drink the juice of the cacti. They get drunk and create all kinds of mischief (Van Huygen 2017).

The description of the underwater panther follows analogous thinking of explaining or characterizing phenomena in natural metaphor.

The underwater panther or Underwater Lynx is known to many First Nations in the eastern half of North America, spanning from subarctic Canada to the southern states. Its appearance varies between cultures. It is most commonly associated with the Ojibwe, who called it *mishipeshu*. This sacred being has the essence of a panther, yet it doesn't always look like one. In many depictions it has horns and a row of sharp spines down its back. It may even have a scaly body. Among some tribes it is allied with the horned serpent or is even conflated with this creature, as in the Iroquois version. As with the horned serpent, the underwater panther is often the enemy of the thunderbird, as its underwater domain is considered oppositional to the sky.

The underwater panther is associated with the violent aspects of water, such as rapids, whirlpools, floods, and large waves. The sound of the rapids and waterfalls is the creature's roar. It uses its long, powerful tail to create disturbances in the water, sometimes overturning boats and drowning people who trespass into its realm. The underwater panther represents forces of nature that are dangerous, but not evil per se. Some tribes regard it as a guardian spirt of the water who may potentially extend its grace to protect humans. The underwater panther is generally respected for its power, and some tribes leave offerings for it. This being is also known as the guardian of copper ore. It is believed to have sunk many boats of those who came to Lake Superior to harvest copper without permission (Frigiola 2019, 25).

Believed to originate among the Cherokee people, the mythical Wampus Cat is a common staple of Appalachian folklore. A shapeshifter, its most common manifestation was as a large, wild cat, but it could also take the shape of a beautiful woman. It was considered a ferocious creature, capable of driving even the bravest of warriors to the brink of insanity. J. K. Rowling's fans may recognize this magical being as a source for the hair that Garrick Ollivander used in the creation of certain magic wands. Fun fact: the word "catawampus," which means "out of alignment" but also "fierce and destructive," arises from this myth. (Life's Abundance 2018)

As discussed earlier, feline characteristics included power and stealth, and by adopting these characteristics—wearing a leopard skin, for example—the individual transformed himself into that animal. This transformation and back again represents the duality factor or the presence of evil within good and vice versa.

Human-felines, warriors or hunters who adopted jaguar or puma dress or accoutrements could be regarded, by themselves and others, as possessing feline souls. Thus, the Apapocuva-Guarani of Brazil regard their neighbors, the Caingang as jaguars. . . . This belief was founded in the Apapocuva concept of the dualistic human soul, where the benign aspect, the *ayvucue*, was associated with the collection and consumption of vegetable foods, and the violent aspect, the *acyigua*, with procurement and consumption of meat. The worst thing that can happen is for a man to have the *acyigua* of a dangerous predator, such as the jaguar, because the *acyigua* always has dominance over the *ayvucue*.

Similar ideas are widespread in South America. In a detailed analysis of Bororo cosmology . . . the spirit form of an animal is the essence of the species, the "jaguar spirit" conceived as "pure being" with which the Bororo say they have a clan or cosmological relationship. Among the Toba, the jaguar is the abode of disembodied evil spirits, and if proper funeral rites are not performed, the dead person might change into a man-jaguar. . . . In Misiones province on the Upper Parana, the Caingua believed that a jaguar that roams the neighborhood of a village burial ground is the transformed spirit of a dead person; among the Chiriguano of Bolivia anyone killed by a jaguar was buried head downwards to forestall his reappearance in jaguar form. . . . When a Bororo dies, it is the duty of a man from the deceased individual's opposite moiety to kill a jaguar (or an animal of the category of which the jaguar is the exemplar), and present it to the deceased's family as partial retribution for their loss. . . .

The potency of the jaguar's spirit is evident in various reactions to the idea of consuming its flesh. Some groups, such as the Abipones, Mbaya, and Mocovi, ate jaguar flesh in order to give themselves strength. . . . In particular the animal's heart or fat was consumed by those who wished to absorb its courage and fierceness . . . and thus to assume the essence of manhood. . . . Similarly, among the Shipibo, the jaguar's predatory powers could be assimilated by drinking its blood. In preparation for warfare and raiding, Carib chiefs and warriors consumed a special manioc-beer (*paiwarri*) that contained the brain, liver, and heart of a jaguar, as these were thought to promote cunning, courage, and energy respectively. . . . (Saunders 1998, 26–28)

The jaguar, however, is not always considered evil. As is the case for ancient Egypt, jaguars are also considered guardians.

In recent times, conservative Maya villages and milpas were believed to have been protected by a jaguar at each world-direction entrance. . . . A jaguar and a snake guard the entrance to the house of the mountain-and-the-valley god of the Ixil Maya. . . . In Colombia, the jaguar is the protector of the maloca longhouse and of the forest for the Desana . . . and the Kogi believe that jaguar-spirits defend archaeological sites. . . . Traditionally, a jaguar skeleton hangs at the door of the Kogi ceremonial house. . . . (Benson 1998, 58)

Benson additionally presents evidence that jaguars were also kept in captivity and there are pottery and stelae depicting a jaguar seated in a man's lap (1998, 60). Benson also points out the ambivalent attitudes toward the jaguar:

In a myth of the Paez, who live near San Agustin, at the beginning of time, a young Paez woman was raped by a jaguar; from this union was born thunder-child, who became a culture-hero. . . . Today, the jaguar-descended thunder-children of the Paez display their male sexual organs to shamans and steal women and carry them off to their dwellings at the bottom of lagoons. . . .

In an Olmec-style cave painting at Oxtotitlan, Guerrero, the tail of a jaguar is placed adjacent to the phallus of a man. . . . A similar theme may be expressed in Argentina, in a Condorhuasi vessel . . . the Inca Pachacuti's vision of the Sun god had the head of a lion jutting out from between his legs. For the Aztec, the jaguar, along with the eagle, wads the symbol of male virility and courage. . . .

The jaguar represents human sexuality and fertility, "mysteries of origin and reproduction, of a dark ancestral past." . . . The power of the jaguar in lowland South American ethnography has a strong sexual component. . . . In northwest Amazonia, the single name by which the shaman and jaguar are designated is a word for cohabitation; both are conceived of as progenitors and procreators, as possessors of sexual energy. . . . Agricultural fertility is implied in the energy. In Tukano thought, as the Sun procreated the earth, the jaguar is procreating, clad in his yellow coat, like a man dominating a woman. . . . (1998, 70–71)

I should also note that the jaguar is a prominent theme in jewelry and pottery (Cordy-Collins 1998, 155–70). Much of the Peruvian pottery referred to by Cordy-Collins depicts the jaguar with his head turned to the side, thus the "backward glance." Many of the pots displaying this also include the San Pedro cactus (*Trichocereus pachanoi*), which contains high concentrations of the hallucinogen mescaline and "structures" called volutes, or entoptic images that go with the hallucinogenic experience. This is shamanic imagery connecting the shaman to the power of the jaguar likely in a similar manner as with Lion-man from Germany dating back thirty to forty thousand years ago.

During our research trip to Mexico we encountered, in a little shop in Oaxaca, the likeness of "jaguar of the backward glance." It is a wood carving, and I wonder if there is a connection with the Peruvian art. The wood carving is about twelve inches tall, with a removable tail, head turned backward, and almost psychedelic decorations perhaps imitating entoptic imagery. We also purchased a jaguar mask from the same artist, and although brightly painted, it did not have the same "entoptic imagery" as the backward-looking cat.

North of Mexico, in the ruins of Pecos Pueblo of New Mexico, there is a burial mound or shrine honoring the mountain lion, apparently the "most important of the Pueblo 'Beast Gods'" (Gunnerson 1998, 228). The question Gunnerson offers is "Was the emphasis on Mountain Lion in the southwestern United States an extension of the 'Feline Deity' cult of Mesoamerica and did it enter the Pueblo area some thousands of years ago as part of a ceremonial complex that included the Plumed Serpent, Quetzalcoatl?" The answer to this is to be found in our ancestors' propensity to explore, and it is not surprising to find many symbols held in common throughout the Americas.

The mountain lion is not the only cat buried in a ceremonial manner. As Mullarkey reports:

In the 1980s, the remains of a young animal were discovered by archaeologists in a burial ground near the Illinois River where Native Americans of the Hopewell Culture had resided approximately two thousand years ago. At the time the remains were labeled as being those of a puppy as the Hopewell did commonly bury their dogs with them. However, decades later, evolutionary anthropologist Angela Perri opened the box and realized immediately that the find had been misidentified. Her instinct was that it was a cat of some kind. Further study revealed that it was a bobcat (*Lynx rufus*) who was only several months old. Amazingly, the bobkitten wore a carefully crafted necklace made of bear teeth and shells.

Photographs of the excavation seem to indicate that the bobcat was intentionally buried with some reverence, as its paws were deliberately placed together. While researchers are unsure whether Native Americans commonly domesticated bobcats or if this was an isolated incident, it's clear that this bobkitten was considered a special animal. Its necklace and carful placement in the burial mound would seem to indicate that it was. Could this be the first pet kitty we know of within what is now the United States?

Artifacts show how prevalent wild cats have been in Native American culture, represented as they were in old drawings as well as by headdresses made from wild cats' skulls. For instance, warriors would paint their faces with whiskers and claws. After European settlement, when *Felis catus* (the good ole house cat to you and me) was introduced, these domesticated felines found a place for themselves among Native Americans much as they had already done among Europeans, partly as rodent control and partly as pets. Some interesting photographs from the early days of photography show Comanche people on horseback with cats perched on their shoulders, although whether this was just an anomaly is hard to ascertain. (2021, 13–14)

I want to turn the reader's attention to an interesting connection between cats in the Americas and cats depicted at an archaeological site in Turkey at Göbekli Tepe. The Huron-Wyandot and Seneca of the northeast United States and Canada connect the panther (mountain lion or puma) to meteors and comets.

The Huron-Wyandot and Seneca regard the panther (meteor/comet) man-being as clairvoyant and prophetic. He is also known as the "the death panther," and, as a guardian figure, is charged with forewarning the people of imminent disaster, whether this be war, famine, or pestilence. . . . It is important to distinguish that the panther man-being is only the "herald of death," not death itself. . . . By means of tobacco invocation, the people can call upon the panther to "turn aside the impending evil" . . . . (Hamell 1998, 268)

Similar to cultures in both the Old and New World, wearing a cat skin, in this case from a panther, bobcat, or lynx, confers power. For the Indians of the Northeast, there "is an implicit hierarchy of potency inherent in felid robes: from bobcat to lynx to panther man-beings" (Hamell 1998, 269).

As mentioned above, I see an interesting connection to the "panther meteor/comet" at the archaeological site of Göbekli Tepe. Approximately 10,900 BCE, a comet entered Earth's atmosphere and broke apart, with large pieces hitting northern Canada, Europe, and other areas. This was devastating to the populations in these areas, certainly from the massive destruction but also because of the mini ice age that followed, called the Younger Dryas, which lasted about 1,300 years. This is likely the event referenced in *Ragnarok: The Age of Fire and Gravel* (Donnelly 2007) and probably the reference to the endless winter in *Game of Thrones*. It is postulated by Collins (2018) and Sweatman (2019) that the archaeological site of Göbekli Tepe in Turkey was perhaps built in memory of this event but also as a ceremonial center, an observatory of sorts, to prevent similar catastrophes from happening in the future or at least as an early warning system. On one of the pillars we see a feline of some sort (with a gaping maw) walking down the pillar, perhaps symbolizing the meteor or comet as it approached the earth—is this the panther meteor/comet or "death panther" of the Seneca? There are also serpents with heads pointed toward the ground as well as the fox and its tail perhaps representing the tail of the comet. This event would have been equally disastrous for cultures in North America and certainly Canada. It is at this point in time (10,900 BCE) that the mastodon and woolly mammoth both disappear from the landscape in North America as well as the Clovis people, whose technology was similar to that of the Solutrean culture of twenty thousand years ago in Western Europe. One has to wonder if the symbolism of the panther in the cultures of Turkey and the northeast United States share that event in their mythology.

Be that as it may, the feline, especially the puma and jaguar, have a special place in Mayan and Aztec cosmology. The puma, according to the research, appears to represent the sun and the Upper World, while the jaguar represents the moon and the Underworld that must be conquered by the sun; this is very similar to the Egyptian narrative with the sun, Re, and the moon analogous to Apepi or Apophis. This idea of celestial conquest by the Mayans and Aztecs, in my opinion, morphs into the cat monsters, likely urban legends, after the Spanish conquistadores and the Catholic Church decimated the native cultures, inflicting disease upon the people and enslaving them, with priests burning their literature and installing the Catholic narrative. Many times, all an oppressed people have is imagination and thoughts of a guardian, a savior, the second coming of Christ (a redo), for example, and revenge or comeuppance, thus the following legends (Taussig 1987).

One of these cat-like creatures is called a *dzulúm* or *balam* which are Mayan words for jaguar. This is a guardian of sorts, and they look after the land. Although a jaguar, it is a shape-shifter and appears in the form of a man with a long beard.

In Chiapas in southern Mexico, bordering Guatemala, the *dzulúm*, depicted as a very large cat that is gray with spots, with white fur on its back, protects its territory in a rather ferocious manner. This *dzulúm* mainly targets women (is this a statement of how the conquistadors treated women?); however, women could also become witches by making a pact with this creature—but they would lose their soul in the process. Out of self-preservation during the early occupation many women likely joined with the conquerors and became turncoats in the minds of the people.

A *nagual* in Mesoamerican folklore is a shaman or sorcerer and shape-shifter who has turned himself into a jaguar. They can do good or evil. This idea of shape-shifting goes back to the Olmec tradition of 1500 BCE. An interesting aspect of the nagual has to do with what is called tonalism in which everyone has a link to an animal spirit, such as a puma or jaguar. "Among the Jacaltek, naguals reinforce indigenism by punishing those who collaborate with non-indigenous Ladinos" (Britannica, "Nagual").

We can see, then, that the feline and its characteristics are appreciated worldwide, as evidenced in cave art, folk tales, and eventually the written word. Such characteristics were first noticed by our ancient, ancient ancestors of the Oligocene and Miocene of thirty to twenty million years ago, and our stress reactions to them were transferred to our genetic code. In modern times stories, narratives, and ritual practices migrated with contemporary humans as they set about colonizing the globe and, because the great cats exist in most areas of the world, these observations and stories were reinforced as they come down to us in folk tales of a more modern form. Originally, strangers were the cats, predators who could get us in the trees and on the ground, and then with urbanization and conquest the evil aspects are transposed to the most vicious predator of them all, the human animal. Urban legends often reference the cat's power especially as a psychological defense against these strangers, for they can act as protectors or guardians as well, turning evil against evil. Later I will investigate these characteristics of the cat and how they are connected to spiritual or otherworldly issues.

6

The Cat in Popular Culture

To this point I have covered a number of characteristics of cats that were perceived as spiritual by our ancient ancestors. Many of these beliefs are still with us today.

In the visual arts the cat takes on a number of different personas and in some cases more than one. The following is, for the most part, a random sample of films and commercials to illustrate how the cat is viewed in modern times. Again, in some cases the cat fills more than one role.

SHAPE-SHIFTING

The following quote is attributed to Pythagoras commenting on Ovid's *Metamorphoses* (Ovid lived from 43 BCE to circa 18 CE and completed *Metamorphoses* in approximately 8 CE).

> *All things are always changing, but nothing dies.*
> *The spirit comes and goes,*
> *Is housed wherever it will, shifts residence*
> *From beast to men, from men to beasts, but always*
> *It keeps on living. As the plant wax*
> *Is stamped with new designs, and is no longer*

What once it was, but changes form, and still
Is plant wax, so do I reach that spirit
Is evermore the same, though passing always
To ever-changing bodies. (Warner 2002, 2)

Our fear of the dark and identification with the cat, as expressed in folklore and myth, has followed us into modern times as evidenced through contemporary cinema. Many such films were aired during the 1920s through the 1950s. For example, *The Cat and the Canary* (1927) is a silent film whose general theme involves Cyrus West, a terminally ill man who is surrounded by a swarm of greedy relatives. He goes insane and dies, but before he does he states that his will, safely locked away, should not be read until twenty years after his death. But, of course, without jeopardy, you have no story. That day arrives, and Annabelle, the most distant of the heirs, inherits all, but a second will is discovered stipulating that if the heir of her uncle's fortune is proven to be insane, then the inheritance would go to the individual on the second will. There is another provision in the will that the players all spend a night in a haunted mansion, a theme occurring frequently in movies from the 1930s through 1970s and even recently.

Bad things begin to happen, like the murder of one of the relatives, the location of hidden hallways, and so on. Another frequent theme, also noted in urban legends (in some renditions of "The Hook"), is the escaped mental patient who, in this case, thinks he is a cat. The "shape-shifting" mental patient is encountered by Paul Jones in one of the hidden hallways. Jones is left for dead but revives just in time to save Annabelle. The "Cat" is caught and unveiled, and they all live happily ever after. To me a better rendition of this original comedy play was done in 1939 staring Bob Hope and Paulette Goddard. In this story we encounter shape-shifting of a psychiatric kind, a split personality, much the same as we encounter with Batman and Catwoman, action heroes or vigilantes, who obviously have problems with their genetic persona and have to assume that of another. In any case, in *The Cat and the Canary*, the cat in this film is a human monster.

Cat People (1942) is another shape-shifting genre with a fashion designer believing she is descended from an ancient clan of cat people who morph into panthers when angered, threatened, or sexually aroused. This story features a love triangle where Irene, the shape-shifter, loves Oliver, and they finally get married—but they never consummate the marriage for fear that, in her animal passion, she would morph into a panther and tear Oliver to shreds. Oliver asks Irene to seek psychiatric help (Dr. Judd), and she does. Oliver, however, suffering from a severe dry spell, falls in heat/love with his assistant, Alice. Irene deduces as much and corners them both, but they escape. Alice, however, gets a whiff of Irene's perfume, and knowing that Irene has an appointment with Dr. Judd, Alice calls and warns that Irene is dangerous. Irene shows up for the appointment, and Dr. Judd, apparently suffering a dry spell as well, kisses Irene quite passionately. Irene morphs into a panther and tears Judd to pieces. She then goes to the zoo and lets a panther out of its cage. The panther then kills Irene and, in its escape, is run over by a passing motorist! Wow, all this is just one hour and thirteen minutes! Oliver and Alice, of course, live happily ever after.

Another shape-shifting movie with a slightly different slant is *A Whisker Away* (2020). This movie is about a girl who morphs into a cat. This animation, called *anime*, is from Japan and involves a junior high school student named Miyo. Hormones are raging at that stage of life, and she has a crush on Kento, a school mate. The shape-shifting part involves a secret mask which, when worn, transforms her into a cat. This is of a similar nature to the movie *The Mask* (1994), with Jim Carrey as a mild-mannered bank clerk who transforms into a maniac with magical powers and a lust for women when he puts on a magical mask of Loki that he finds floating in the river. Anyway, Miyo uses the mask to transform into a cat, thinking this is the way to get Kento's attention. But, alas, she can't keep putting on the mask lest she remain a cat forever.

Stephen King's name is synonymous with horror and bad decisions, his storylines leading to violent mishap. In his screenplay *Sleepwalkers* (1992), a mother and son move into a town populated by shape-shifting cat-like monsters who roam the town at night feeding off the energy of young women. But there is a twist here in that normal cats in town aid in dealing with the monster shape-shifters.

Shape-shifting, then, a common theme in folklore worldwide, has carried into modern times, likely reinforced by the witch hunt craze of Europe during the Middle Ages and also in early New England. These stories speak to that part of us, chosen as a survival mechanism millions of years ago—fear of the dark, of the bogeyman lurking in the shadows, or of being eaten, thus leaving your world behind.

But no discussion of shape-shifting is complete without mentioning the most modern rendition as encountered in Catwoman, as mentioned earlier, which matches our interpretation of werewolves and witches, and the connection to psychopathology and the use of mind-altering substances. Let's first get the mind-altering substances out of the way.

Mind-altering substances as connected to numerous religions, for example, Hinduism, Buddhism, Judaism, Christianity, and Islam, were kept out of the literature by most historians and anthropologists until late in the twentieth century for political reasons. The rituals and use of such substances were deemed secret and not to be discussed lest they reveal where some of our ideas about life, otherworldly affairs, and technology came from, or perhaps we would all turn into drug addicts. To think that mind-altering drugs were in any way important in the development of culture was deemed preposterous (Rush 2013)! Well, these scholars were wrong. The sensation of shape-shifting could be facilitated using a number of plants, including henbane (*Hyoscyamus niger*), jimsonweed (*Datura stramonium*), belladonna (*Atropa belladonna*), and mandrake (*Mandragora officinarum*), to name a few that contain scopolamine, which can be consumed orally or through oils rubbed into the skin or mucus membrane. Witches' ointment, made from belladonna and fat (the Catholic Church says baby fat), was inserted in the vaginal opening, giving us the witch flying on a broom, likely the instrument for inserting the ointment. The broom was characterized as a woman's tool, while the man's tool was a pitchfork—thus the witch and the devil. Scopolamine taken in sufficient quantity not only produces a sensation of flying, but shape-shifting as well, for example, as a wolf or cat. I suppose anything is possible, but I suspect the better explanation for shape-shifting experiences were brought on by psychosis or artificial psychosis through powerful plants and fungi. Remember that our ancient ancestors strongly identified with specific animals they hunted or that hunted them, like the bear, the lion, and the wolf. So turning into these animals was preconditioned by our ancestors as a gate to power during their rites and rituals.

Regarding psychosis and the split personality, superheroes all have alter egos, the "shape" they shift into when duty calls. Most of these superheroes are men, but carefully inserted women began making the scene with Wonder Woman in 1941 (Superman first appeared in 1938), probably evolving from the efforts of women working in factories, building tanks and such, during WWII. Wonder Woman is pretty much the counterpart of Superman, but her powers come from being born on Earth among the Amazons, a tribe of women enslaved by men because they would not fight with them against an enemy. Wonder Woman has powers above that of mortal man and escapes into our world to save it from evil. Superman is from another planet and his great strength, which allows him to be "faster than a speeding bullet" or "leap tall building in a single bound," comes from his otherworldly birth. We can somewhat excuse these two superheroes from the bane of psychosis, but Batman and Catwoman we cannot. In fact, these two create more carnage, with great passion, than the villains they pursue.

Catwoman (2004) stars Halle Berry as Selina Kyle, a flight attendant who survives a plane crash. She has amnesia but retained memories of her father's store and the cats she cherished (there are different origins, however) and she becomes Catwoman. According to the critics, the movie was a flop. The original story began in the 1940s and portrayed her as a thief (a "cat" burglar) and archenemy of Batman (a flying "mouse"!)—she is a villain whose character evolves, certainly, but the fact remains we have an individual similar to Batman with a split personality, who is one minute in society and in the next outside it stealing precious jewels. What Catwoman symbolizes is the evil in society masquerading as normal and unassuming. There is a likeness here to the shaman who dons the jaguar skin, consumes some hallucinogenic potion (San Pedro, for example) and flies, often inflicting great harm on enemies. But this power can be used for healing purposes—Catwoman can be nurturing.

I am not sure Sylvester James Pussycat, Sr., from Warner Brothers, in their *Looney Tunes* cartoons, qualifies as a monster; he is more of a comic villain for kids, perhaps preparing them for the real world. He officially shows up in 1945 in *Life with Feathers*. Most of the cartoons, however, involve Sylvester attempting to eat Tweety Pie, of "I tawt I taw a Puddy Tat" fame. Recall what I said about cats and our ancient ancestors, who, in this case, are symbolized as a yellow canary.

THE TRICKSTER

Although the trickster is a common theme in folktales and legends, I haven't found the trickster cat popular in modern cinema. For the most part the cat is neutral or used as a prop, something to divert attention or draw attention to some issue. A trickster cat appears in cartoon form in 1919, with the release of a film starring Felix the Cat. Felix qualifies as a trickster because he causes trouble, like Loki, but reaches into his bag of tricks and narrowly escapes detection, often trapping the bad guys.

And certainly, we have the Cheshire Cat in *Alice in Wonderland* (1951), that memorable Walt Disney cartoon based on Lewis Carroll's works. If parents only knew back then that Alice was on powerful hallucinogens—well, that's another story. In any case, the Cheshire Cat is pink with purple stripes and glowing yellow eyes. And, of course, he (yes, it's a tomcat, sort of) has that famous smile characteristic of your average car salesman or politician. The Cheshire Cat is a troublemaker, that's for sure, but he also acts as Alice's guide.

CONNECTION TO THE UNDERWORLD

Cats since ancient times, especially in Egypt, have been connected to the Underworld, often as guardians. *Fallen* (1998), for example, is not your typical horror film, nor does the featured feline play much of a role—until the very last minute of the movie. The story is about a detective (Denzel Washington) investigating recent murders who notices a similarity to those committed by a recently executed serial killer. Not to ruin the punch line, but the cat, at the end, hints at the identity of the individual behind the recent murders, with the cat acting as a connection between the two worlds.

In *Constantine* (2005), starring Keanu Reeves, the cat plays the role of a facilitator or even a guide during his passage into hell in order to vanquish demons. Apparently cats and demons share at least one thing in common: they are both half in and half out of this world.

Haunted houses and cats, especially black ones, were popular symbols of evil and Underworld activity, a belief left over from the Middle Ages. *The Legend of Hell House* (1973) is a good example of such symbolism. The plot centers around three "scientists" attempting to prove life after death, and, of course, the experiments have to occur in a haunted house, not a clean lab somewhere, like a hospital or university perhaps. Life after death requires an Underworld of sorts, and the cat seems to fulfill that part of the symbolism. Although more of a prop, the connection is clear enough.

MATCHMAKER

In *Bell, Book and Candle* (1958), Kim Novak is part of an urban coven of witches who falls in love with James Stewart, which is taboo. (Why taboo? This is prejudice against non-witches, muggles in the Harry Potter series.) The downside to the movie is the annoying music, but the bright side is Pyewacket, the nosey cat who helps foster the relationship, along with the love magic, of course.

Lady and the Tramp (1955), a full-length Disney cartoon, is mainly about dogs, but, without the aid of Si and Am, "Siamese, if you please!," Lady would never have met Tramp.

ADVENTURE, COMPANIONSHIP, AND BONDING

Harry and Tonto (1974) is about a retired teacher, Harry (played by Art Carney), who, with his companion Tonto (played by a short-haired ginger), is moving across the United States in search of a new home. Instead of bonding to another human, Harry bonds with the cat, who shows loyalty and a warmth toward Harry, obviously something lacking in his life, and, apparently for Harry, something only Tonto could fill.

A Street Cat Named Bob (2016) is based on a true story of a homeless street musician and drug addict who befriends a cat named Bob, a ginger, of course, who is injured and in need of care. James takes on the task. Caring is a spiritual issue and James, who never cared much for anyone but himself, found that the experience of caring for Bob and the bond they formed, pushed him to mend his ways. It is a touching story and there is a truth here—cats show an amazing sense of caring, not for groups of people, but individuals and other cats that *they* choose.

One of the more recent cartoon adventure movies is *Shrek* (2001). The cat, Puss in Boots, shows up in Shrek 2 (2004), voiced by Antonio Banderas. Similar to Felix the Cat, Puss in Boots is a trickster, but in this rendering, he, along with Donkey (voiced by Eddie Murphy), helps

Shrek (voiced by Mike Myers) find his true love, a princess who was transformed into an ogre (of the same lineage as Shrek) by an evil fairy godmother.

There are a number of Walt Disney films featuring cats and dogs who go on great adventures, sometimes unwillingly. Usually there is humor, but more important is the companionship and bonding that occurs during the adventures. Some of these Disney movies include *The Aristocats* (1970), *The Incredible Journey* (1963), *Oliver & Company* (1988), and *Homeward Bound: The Incredible Journey* (1993).

One should not neglect the Tarzan character (created by Edgar Rice Burroughs) and his connection to lions. The lion's name was Jad-bal-ja for those who have read Burroughs's work or followed the comic books. The character of Jad-bal-ja, the Golden Lion, is a companion. Over time, the basic theme was transferred to movies and comic books. One of the earliest movies was the 1927 silent movie, *Tarzan and the Golden Lion*, which was an adaptation of the book series, *Tarzan of the Apes*. The lion also appears as a recurring character in Filmation's animated series *Tarzan, Lord of the Jungle* (1976–1981). Numerous Tarzan films have appeared over the years. The main characteristic of the lion, however, is power. Tarzan, the main character, is likewise powerful—as powerful as the lion, and this can, I suppose, be credited to Tarzan's primitive upbringing and long relationship with our primate cousins, chimps and gorillas.

Circus acts involving lions and tigers have been popular; as you recall, big cats played a role in dispatching evil Christians at least two thousand years ago, and certainly "criminals" years before that. In the more recent circus acts, we encounter the lion tamer, with his or her whip and chair, and a well-fed lion, forced to humiliate itself by jumping up on stools or through rings of fire. Lions and tigers are not domesticated animals; they did not choose to hang out with humans and eat mice. Most of the traveling circuses are gone now, a thing of the past. Siegfried and Roy, mentioned earlier, represent perhaps the last of their kind with their main attraction being "man conquering nature," with nature, and its power, represented by these majestic animals that will eat you if they get the chance.

PROP

Cats are many times used in movies as a prop or as something that distracts or points to an important issue. In these cases, the cat's appearance could be achieved by any number of animals or objects and thus their presence is superfluous. In many Egyptian tomb scenes, a cat is often shown seated (sometimes tied) under the chair of the wife of a pharaoh. The legs of the chair under which the lady sits often have the feet of a cat, probably a lion. The cat doesn't need to be there and probably, in a minor way, represents power, authority, companionship, or even protection.

In the horror movie *Alien* (1979), Jonesy the cat represents loyalty and the screen writers' need to place Ripley (Sigourney Weaver) in rather constant jeopardy as she goes out of her way to rescue Jonesy. Of course, there is always the reality that Ripley would be totally alone in space without a companion once the monster is dispatched. Solitary confinement in a space capsule would be as cruel as solitary confinement in prison.

In *That Darn Cat* (1965), the Siamese cat does have a purpose and that is sending an SOS to FBI agents concerning a kidnapped bank teller. A fun movie but, again, the cat is mainly a prop—not a monster, trickster, shape-shifter, matchmaker, or agent of both worlds.

Inside Llewyn Davis (2013) is another movie where a lost cat (once again a ginger) is a prop, providing a sort of backstory to simply move the film along.

Mrs. Norris, the cat of *Harry Potter* (2001–2011) fame, belongs to Argus Filch, the macabre and rather bad-tempered caretaker of Hogwarts. Once again, Mrs. Norris is a prop but also acts as a warning that evil is afoot—but she is not essential to the storyline.

WARNING

We are all familiar with *The Matrix* (1999) starring Keanu Reeves. The cat in this movie appears only once, maybe twice. When trying to get back to the Nebuchadnezzar, Neo notices a cat walk by a doorway. He looks away, then looks back and sees the same cat walk by the doorway. He mentions this to the others and they respond, "déjà vu," signaling to them that the powers that be were on to them and changed the coding in the matrix. They get trapped, of course; you don't have a good story without danger.

In the flick *When a Stranger Calls* (2006), a teenager is babysitting in a remote house. The symbolism here is typical and represents the dark forest, the haunted house, the remote island, and so on, setting the scene for bad things to come. The cat—a black cat in this case—shows up unexpectedly as a prop to keep the audience on edge, but it also acts as a symbol for evil, a warning of bad things to happen in the future. The cat itself is not evil and serves to play on cultural myths and superstitions.

The cat certainly has a bad reputation in popular myth as evil and up to no good. Our cats are always up to no good, pushing objects off tables, opening closet doors and walking away with whatever they can drag out. (To answer your question, yes, they can open doors. We had to switch out all our lever door handles for traditional round door-knobs, and, without an opposable thumb, they are now locked out.) They have yet to reveal their demonic side. In any case, in *Eye of the Cat* (1969) we encounter a bevy of unfriendly cats who will inherit all the cat lady's money and property, much to the chagrin of her nephew and his girlfriend. The cats not only serve as warning signs, but also actually impede the greedy nephew's objective of having his aunt alter her will.

In the animated film *Coraline* (2009), we encounter hidden passage-ways that lead to a world that is a mirror of the main character's life.

Though she is entranced at first, the black cat serves to warn Coraline, an eleven-year-old girl, about the dark nature of this "new world." This dark nature is really about that part of her, symbolized as the hidden door, and what possibilities lay beyond, both good and evil.

FOOD AND OIL/FAT

There aren't many films available portraying cats being eaten or their fat or oil used for cosmetics. But there is one, *The Book of Eli* (2010). The general plot is that Eli (Denzel Washington) survives a catastrophic event and has a Bible that Carnegie (Gary Oldman) desperately wants to possess because he thinks it is magical and will help in his desire to control people. The cat shows up in three scenes. In the first two scenes (actually the first minutes of the film), Eli kills and then cooks and eats the cat, saving its fat/oil for potential barter down the way. He comes into a town wanting to charge his iPod and attempts to barter the cat oil with the merchant. While waiting, he goes to the bar across the street, in which he pushes a cat off the bar (the cat's third and last scene) and ends up in a battle with patrons. He thinks he is invincible due to an "inner voice" and, of course, kills or seriously maims his attackers. As the story moves along, he turns out not to be invincible. He is blind (the Bible he has is in braille) and he dies, but not before he verbally dictates the Bible to Lombardi, the leader of the sanctuary on Alcatraz.

There are lots and lots of films featuring cats. All fit into one or more of the categories listed above. Here is a partial list:

Hocus Pocus (1993)
Stuart Little (1999)
Cats and Dogs (2001)
Garfield (2004)
Grumpy Cat's Worst Christmas Movie Ever (2014)

Cats (2019)

Pet Sematary (1989)

The Secret Life of Pets (2016)

The Curse of the Cat People (1944)

The Leopard Man (1943)

The Mummy (1932, 1999)

The Tomb of Ligeia (1964)

Willard (1971)

Drag Me to Hell (2009)

The Voices (2014)

A Girl Walks Home Alone at Night (2014)

Blood Feast (1972)

The Corpse Grinders (1971)

Crimes of the Black Cat (1972)

The Shadow of the Cat (1961)

Strays (1991)

Tales from the Darkside: The Movie (1990)

The cinema, then, offers a number of spiritual themes corresponding to those noted in chapter 4. Cats have power; they can shape-shift and inflict harm. They also can act as warning signals (guardians) in the face of impending danger. They likewise show loyalty through bonding to specific individuals, and also suggest, as matchmakers, the issue of fertility and primal desires. And, if demons have a spiritual quality, then, because they live in two worlds, the demon cat of the cinema fulfills that role as well.

COMMERCIALS

Product commercials have been kind to cats. They are used, often as a prop, to sell everything from cat food (all brands) and trucks (Chevy Silverado) to mortgages.

Large cats like lions and tigers, however, have a lasting connection to many products. Tony the Tiger, for example, made his debut for Kellogg's in 1953 with Kellogg's Frosted Flakes. The idea, I suppose, was to attach the power of the tiger to the effects of eating sugar-frosted corn flakes. Although the target audience was likely children, parents eat breakfast cereal, too, and the tiger probably appealed to the parent's need for power as well. Symbols are powerful and no one seemed to question the connection between corn flakes and tigers. The appeal is the cuteness of the tiger and the fact the kids would eat the cereal, the corn, and all that sugar. The food industry is aware of our addiction to sugar, fat, and salt, rare but sought-after substances needed by our ancient ancestors.

And then there is "Put a tiger in your tank," the slogan for Esso motor oil and gasoline that came out in the 1950s, but really took hold in the wake of super cars like the Mustang, GTO, and so on beginning around 1963. This tiger didn't have a specific name but offered a catchy metaphor fostering the belief that Esso gas would provide *more* power. Along with the slogan, you could buy a toy tiger tail to hang out of your gas tank—very clever advertising.

Closely related to the tiger in your tank are Tiger Paws, by Uniroyal, tires that were first introduced on the Pontiac GTO in 1964. The main theme was traction and more power moving forward rather than spinning your wheels and, of course, control of that power when sliding around corners.

Then there is the cheetah, "Chester Cheetah," illustrated (incorrectly, I might add) on Frito Lay's Cheetos. The original mascot was a mouse, but a mouse (except Mighty Mouse) does not convey much in the way of power—power and performance sells, thus the Cheetah. The Cheetah is a short-faced cat; it doesn't have the long muzzle of the lion and is even shorter than that of the leopard.

We also have sportswear with the brand name Puma, which hit the market place in 1948 with the Atom soccer shoe. Today they make all kinds of sportswear, from sweatpants to accessories for training and fitness.

LOCAL INTEREST

Cats, however, have a more hidden presence outside of movies and commercials. For community interest, local newspapers often include stories of animals who were rescued or who rescued others. This would include the cat who, in one story, entered a library, befriended the librarian, and decided to stay. Now the cat, curled up at the entrance, greets visitors and provides a calming atmosphere.

Then there is the story of the cat who entered a police station and immediately started to rid the place of rats, placing them on the captain's desk after each kill. These stories and many more can be found in *The Cats of America* (Mullarkey 2021). My favorite is the mention of "Robo Kitties," or robot cats available in nursing homes and other facilities (Mullarkey 2021, 124). I googled robo cats and, indeed, you can buy one of these for around $140.00 in U.S. currency, although less expensive models are available. These cute, cuddly automatons will meow, purr, walk, avoid objects, and so on. The human ability to fantasize and engage analogous thinking has no limits.

CARS, CATS, AND POWER

The ability to move rapidly in the face of danger is important to all animals. Reaction time is always paramount. Cats are quick with incredible power released in microseconds. Cats have sacrificed endurance for initial speed, for, as in any combat situation, the longer it goes on the higher the probability of injury to both sides. Humans want power and speed and so we, once again, borrowed them, first from horses and horse-drawn chariots, and then attached them to vehicles with engines measured in "horsepower." Over the years that horsepower has been connected to cats, symbols that define the *nature* of that horsepower. The automobile that perhaps first comes to mind is the Jaguar, first available in 1935, manufactured by the Swallow Sidecar Company.

Today the icon is owned by Tata Motors but manufactured by Jaguar Land Rover (Motor Car 2023). If you want a very fast, quality ride, connected to the name of a cat, Jaguar is the way to go.

A very fast, powerful micro-muscle car, first produced in 1964 by Rootes Group of British fame, is the Sunbeam Tiger. This very light vehicle had a small block V-8 under the hood; I don't think I have ridden in anything faster. The desire for small muscle cars for American consumers had its beginning in the 1950s with the Chevy Corvette and Ford Thunderbird. These were expensive, but in the 1960s the competition for the muscle car market allowed production of cars with a more modest price tag, and, of course, financing. Once again, cats were connected to horsepower—in most cases. We have the Mercury Cougar, first available in 1967, with a 390 CC V-8 delivering 320 HP (the same motor was available for the Mustang). The Buick Wildcat first debuted in 1963 with 325 HP.

The Mercury Bobcat (1974–1980) and the Lynx (1981–1987) were not muscle cars, and the Bobcat was based on the Ford Pinto—an insult to the Bobcat, I might add. In fact, the Pinto was considered a rolling "death trap," a very poorly manufactured automobile (Dowie 1977). The Lynx wasn't dangerous to drive, but it wasn't powerful either. For the Mercury Bobcat, it did live up to one characteristic of the cats that ate our ancestors—it was dangerous!

One final mention is the Bill Thomas Cheetah, produced from 1963–1966. Definitely a muscle car, the Cheetah was basically built for drag racing, and only a handful were manufactured.

7

Felines and the Cosmos

Felines feature prominently in cosmology and their identification in the heavens must have a long, long season. We saw those cats among the cave paintings at cave sites at Chauvet (thirty-two thousand years ago) and Lascaux (twenty thousand years ago). The feline is also an important symbol at Göbekli Tepe (around 9600 BCE). We do not know which star clusters they gestalted into animal images (if any) but at least at Göbekli Tepe, we know the positioning of the megalithic architecture was altered every generation or so when they built a new site to line up with certain stars, their position altered due to precession.

The field of archaeoastronomy emerged as we began to see connections between megalithic structures and their orientation to the heavens. For our ancestors, nighttime was dark and often dangerous with predators in search of a meal. Perhaps standing vigil, watching for danger, they noted changes in the heavens as the dots of light migrated across the night sky, some very rapidly, while the moon changed its shape. Our ancestors noticed patterns, and these have been preserved for us as counts on bone (Marshack 1991, 33–56). As time went on these lights and changes demanded an understanding, a story or narrative as to the meaning of this movement in the skies. All they knew was what they experienced day after day: the sun, moon, rain, winds, the actions and behaviors of our friends and relatives, and the behavior of animals and the coming and going of plants. These experiences and the assigned names and meanings were transposed to the heavens. These narratives also bound us to our deceased human relatives, the gods and goddesses, and our animal relatives who were also our clan names, the lion, the bear, our ancient, ancient ancestors. Many myths indicate that at one time we were the tiger, the lion, and the bear; Buddha had several past lives, some as animals.

The star narratives are a mirror informing how we think and organize our universe. In a dualistic universe, when we enter the field of time, one should not be surprised that we conceptualize two worlds (at least), an Upper and a Lower, and we stand between the two (so that is actually three worlds), with the in-between a mirror of Upper and Lower.

Cats have a special place in cosmology, with the best known the Sphinx of Egyptian fame. Much controversy surrounds this monolith with some Egyptologists—especially those who, in their writings, dogmatically committed themselves to a date corresponding to the building of the Great Pyramid of Khufu around 2600 BCE. There may be good reasons to believe that this monument is much, much older and was perhaps built at a time period when the Sphinx was aligned with the constellation of Leo, around 10,500 BCE. This is possibly connected, in some way, to the building of the site of Göbekli Tepe in Turkey, which may be a reminder of the catastrophic event of 10,900 BCE that decimated much of North America and Northern Europe—lots of "maybe" and "perhaps." For the relatives of the Olmecs, Mayans, and Aztecs, conflicts in the heavens may mirror this event as well. It is no surprise that one of the basic cosmological narratives for the Maya and Aztecs concerns an ongoing war between the sun and the moon.

ANCIENT MAYA AND AZTEC

Among with Maya their observations of the sun and moon were described in metaphor as a battle.

Thompson (1960, 11, 231) notes that the widespread Mesoamerican belief that eclipses represent fights between the sun and the moon is not shared by the Maya; nevertheless, a number of Maya accounts use this explanation for eclipses. The Tzeltal, Tzutujil, and the Pokomchi believe that eclipses are caused by fights between the sun and the moon. Pre-Columbian Aztec images suggest that the sun and the moon are fighting during eclipses (Milbrath 1995b, 1997). Images that account for eclipses as fights suggests an understanding that the relative position of the sun and the moon causes the eclipse.

Some Tojolabal accounts say that the sun and the moon come together in a sexual union at the time of the eclipse (Baez-Jorge 1988, 244). Others say that the moon is furious and bites the sun during solar eclipse, but they attribute lunar eclipses to an attack by black ants (Illia Najera Coronado 1995, 323). Such a distinction between the causes of lunar and solar eclipses suggests observations made of the relative positions of the sun and the moon, for the new moon passing in front of the sun makes it look as if the moon takes a bite out of the sun. But because lunar eclipses occur when the sun and the moon are at opposite sides of the sky at the full moon, the Tojolabal invoke a third party as the cause of the lunar eclipse. "A number of Maya communities say that the eclipsed body is ill in some respect, considerably weakened or dying . . ." (Milbrath 1999, 26–27).

This great variability suggests significant isolation between the various Mayan communities, perhaps before but certainly after the Europeans showed up bringing disease, war, and a reduction of the population. In any case, Milbrath (1999, 94–95) has more to say about the puma and jaguar:

The puma has a golden coat and is active primarily in the daytime, like the sun. In fact, solar puma can be seen in a puma with a crown of solar rays at Teotihuacan (Miller 1973, fig. 289). The sun God sits with a puma on a throne in the Codex Laud (14), a codex that blends central Mexican and Mayan traits. The solar symbolism of pumas may have extended into the Maya area. Just as the sun has higher status than the moon in contemporary Mayan accounts, the Tzotzil give the puma higher status than the jaguar (Braakhuis 1987, 247) . . . .

Feline thrones are quite common in Maya imagery, and many thrones clearly show a spotted jaguar pelt covering the throne (Fig. 3.11e, Pls. 5, 7, 17). At Palenque, the Palace Oval Tablet shows Pascal receiving his crown on a throne representing a feline with two heads (Robertson 1985a, fig. 91). Although spots are not represented, the head ornaments clearly designate the Water-Lilly jaguar [. . .]

The jaguar is nocturnal and likes to swim and fish, thus it is naturally linked with the moon and the watery underworld.

The Water-Lilly jaguar, by the way, connects the jaguar with water and the moon and ". . . the jaguar's nocturnal nature suggests a natural connection with the moon, and the jaguar spots suggest the stars of the night sky" (Milbrath 1999, 94–95). With the puma-jaguar dichotomy we see the duality in nature, where you cannot have good without evil, just as you can't have day without night. The jaguar, however, is, for the most part, connected to power, to shape-shifting shamans and priests and rulers taking on the spiritual essence of these powerful cats. The theme of the sun taking over the moon during eclipses and during the moon's phases was interpreted as a war, and it may be that the frequent wars, often engaged during the dry summer months, were "enacted" because of this mythic theme. The Popol Vuh, which translates into "council book," is a creation story, written shortly after the initial European invasion, filled with astronomical data regarding the sun, moon, and Venus wherein the Jaguar and its characteristics are quite evident (Tedlock 1996).*

---

*For a synopsis of the Popol Vuh see Miller and Taube 1993, 134–37.

MIDDLE EAST

Middle Eastern cosmology, through the written word, allows a more certain or detailed connection to cats. As mentioned, some of the earliest renderings of felines in art are to be found in those caves in France and Spain. But they are difficult to interpret, although I will return to the shaman found at Lascaux shortly.

Early on in Mesopotamian art (4000–3000 BCE) we encounter numerous wild animals:

> Interest in wild animals, and particularly in features like horns, wings, and claws that were considered especially dangerous or powerful [...], is characteristic of ancient Near Eastern art of all periods, dating back at least to the Neolithic period. At the site of Göbekli Tepe, stone pillars were carved in relief with images of animals such as vultures and foxes, while at Çatalhöyük, plaster installations of animal teeth and horns and wall paintings of animals, including one of an enormous bull, were found in domestic spaces. Contrary to what we might expect of the peoples who first domesticated many animals and plants, it is not the inner controlled and domesticated world that they chose to represent but the outer, wild world. During the Uruk period, the lion and bull became especially prominent in the art of the ancient Near East and first began to be used in images expressing the power of rulers. Images of lions were also used in protective contexts, and were set up in pairs to guard passageways into royal and ritual spaces [....] Conflict between two or more powerful creatures is a recurring theme in ancient Near Eastern art [....] Fierce animals shown locked in combat were perhaps meant to embody strong opposing forces in nature. (The Met 2014)

The ancient Mesopotamians, however, had a number of composite lion gods. In literature, the lion is a favorite metaphor for warlike kings and fierce deities, especially Ninurta or Inanna. A popular saying was: "He who seizes the tail of a lion will drown in the river; he who seizes the tail of a fox will be saved" (Black and Green 2014, 118).

A duo, La-tarak and Lulal, have been described as follows:

> Either Lulal is a Sumerian god and La-tarak is an Akkadian name for the same deity, or the two gods were originally distinct but closely related. In the later second millennium BC Lulal and La-tarak were treated as a pair, and in Neo-Assyrian times figurines of them were buried at doorways as magically protective deities. It has been suggested that they might be represented visually at this time as respectively an anthropomorphic god with raised fist ... and a lion-headed human-bodied figure cloaked in a lion's pelt and carrying a whip. In a magical text they are listed among deities protective against witchcraft. (Black and Green 2014, 116)

There is also a lion-centaur found in the Assyrian art: "The so-called lion-centaur of Middle Assyrian and Neo-Assyrian art is a hybrid creature with a lion's lower body (including all four legs), and the head, upper body and arms and hands of a man. The creature's name was *urmahlullu*, 'lion-man'" (Black and Green 2014, 119).

We also encounter the lion-humanoid:

> In Kassiet, Neo-Assyrian and Seleucid art we find, if rarely, a minor deity (in horned cap) human above the waist but with two lion legs and lion's hind-quarters, including a curled-over lion's tail. Figures of this type are sometimes paired with those of a bull-man and the creature may similarly be associated with Samas (Utu). In any event he seems to be a late invention based upon the bull-man and scorpion-man. He is a protective figure. His Akkadian name seems to have been *uridimmu*, which could be translated as "mad lion" (literally, "mad canine"). (Black and Green 2014, 122)

A rather unusual monstrous bird was called Imdugud (Anzu):

Imdugud is probably the correct reading of a Sumerian name of a monstrous bird who is called Anzu in Akkadian. Envisaged as bird-like but having the head of a lion, and of gigantic size so that the flapping of its wings could cause whirlwinds and sandstorms, the Imdugud was probably originally a personification of an atmospheric force (its name is used to write a word meaning "fog" or "mist"). Other descriptions of the Anzu indicate that it had a beak "like a saw," and so presumably a bird's head. In Neo-Assyrian art, a monster combining bird and lion elements may be the Anzu or the Asakku (Asag). (Black and Green 2014, 107)

For the Mesopotamians, Greeks, and Romans, and even to this day we see the constellation Leo the lion as prominent in the myths. Looking north in the night sky, locate the Big Dipper (Ursa Major) with Leo the lion just south while Orion is in the west. Keep in mind that the view of specific constellations depends on where you are standing. For example, the constellations available to a viewer in Chiapas (Mexico) will be quite different from what I would see living in northern California.

The constellation of Leo is thought to be one of the earliest constellations recognized by the Mesopotamians. Others, including Persians (Ser or Shir), Turks (Artan), Syrians (Aryo), Jews (Arye), and East Indians (Simha), all reference the lion. In any case, Leo enters the written record in Mesopotamia around 4000 BCE. But there is another feline of importance to the Mesopotamians, and that is the sky-panther. Collins (2018, 55), referring to symbols at the archaeological site at Göbekli Tepe, Turkey, comments:

Seemingly, on entering Enclosure H, the shaman, initiate, or celebrant would have approached between its twin central pillars, where, on the eastern example at least, the carved relief of a panther-like beast could have been seen to rear up at them. Standing here they would have been able to project their mind through the circular aperture of the porthole stone toward the realm of the dead, which was presumably guarded by just such a creature. If so, then panther-like creatures of Enclosure H are almost certainly proto-forms of mulUD.KA.DUH.A (Akkadian Ukaduhha or Kadduhha), the Mesopotamian sky panther-griffin, whose name, as we have already seen, means "constellation [MUL] of the storm demon with the gaping mouth." It was an asterism made up of key stars of Cygnus, along with others from the neighboring constellation of Cepheus.

For peoples of the Middle East, the constellations, or how they imagined the constellations, fit into their lives in at least two ways. One was a reference to the gods living in the sky and their characteristics. The other reference had to do with agriculture, seasonal changes, and when to plant and harvest. The ancients were astute observers of nature, especially the night sky when there was little to do but watch the changing positions. As the imagined constellations moved across the night sky, they informed as to when the rains would come, when planting should begin and end, and so on. For the Mesopotamians, and apparently until the Greeks, death meant a trip to the Underworld (Kur), a holding tank controlled by the goddess Ereshkigal, and that was it. This to me appears a bit strange as there is circumstantial evidence that the concept of a soul that moves to the heavens at death seems to have been a part of the metaphysics conceptualized by the early shamans who painted in those caves in France and Spain. The sky-panther mentioned above would suggest a connection with Göbekli Tepe (and possibly the Seneca). Again, I refer to Collins (2018, 270–71):

Between 15,750 and 12,750 BCE the stars occupying the position of the northern celestial pole were those of Cygnus, and even in this age the constellation was almost certainly seen in terms of a celestial bird. By virtue of its astronomical position, its stars would have been believed to guard and even control the turning of the heavens as a deity in its own right. In the earliest days of Egypt this bird would become a creator in the form of a falcon, celebrated in what might have been the first primeval enclosure ever built in the country. To get a further idea of this very ancient belief in a controlling force of the heavens in the form of a bird, we must examine a painted relief to be found on the northern wall of an almost inaccessible pit known as the Well Shaft, or the Shaft of the Dead Man, in the famous caves at Lascaux in the Dordogne region of southern France.

Here among the ice-age art created by accomplished Solutrean artists circa 16,500–15,000 BCE, we see a bird perched on a pole, above which is a male human figure with the head of a bird. He leans at an unnatural angle as if falling backward and, curiously, has an erect penis, just like the headless figure on Göbekli Tepe's Vulture Stone (Pillar 43). This is almost certainly a sign that he is a shaman in deathlike trance, for men can have erections in the early stages of an altered state induced by hallucinogens, just as they come close to the point of death.

To the figure's right is a large bovine, a bison most probably, with a spear in its back and blood and guts spilling from its underside. Professor Michael Rappenglueck of the University of Munich has identified this painted fresco, found in the Shaft of the Dead Man, situated in the most northerly part of the cave complex, as a representation of the area of the sky occupied by the stars making up the Summer Triangle.

What Collins is referring to is the soul, as a separate feature of the human body, that leaves the body at death and goes in the direction of the heavens, more specifically north toward the constellation of Cygnus, at least at that time period, a metaphysics shared with many people in

Eurasia to this day. My question is why, if this was a significant part of the mythic narrative of people 15,000 BCE—as suggested at Göbekli Tepe (9600 BCE) and Çatalhöyük (7100 BCE), *and* ancient Egypt—is it missing from the metaphysics of Samarians, Babylonians, and Assyrians only to reemerge at the time of the Greeks? It seems we are missing a large chunk of information or perhaps the interpretation offered by Collins is wrong. But there are other interpretations of the Shaft of the Dead Man.

Some scholars (Magli 2009, 9–12) have suggested that the Shaman (Dead Man) represents Orion and to his right is the constellation of Taurus, while slightly above and to the left would be Leo, and to his left and above would be Cygnus. Cygnus would be northeast of Ursa Major and on the horizon if it was to be seen in conjunction with Orion, Taurus, and Leo. The cave image is very suggestive of this arrangement as seen by our ancestors, although we do not know the names given to the star clusters. Cygnus, as some sort of bird, is obvious enough, Taurus possibly, but Leo is not in the picture and is speculation. However if the shaman was seen as an animal master, which appears to be the case at Les Trois-Frères, then they likely had numerous analogies and comparisons between human activity and the actions of the cosmos—this would include names for stars and star configurations. The human world, in their mind, extended into the heavens, and the forms the star clusters took were likely based on what they knew: the bear, the felines, the bull, themselves, and so on. But those likely imaginings represented power, clearly denoted on the faces or postures of animals carved into the pillars at Göbekli Tepe. Because we do not have a narrative outside of the ones we invent, we do not know for sure what these animals symbolized, including the lion, but I think it safe to say they represent celestial power and likely celestial geography. At Göbekli Tepe we could be witnessing symbols of a catastrophic event in the past (10,900 BCE) and a warning of what is to come. This event of 10,900 BCE wiped out thousands of people, with isolated survivors, but it was likely a key factor in the development of sedentary agriculture and the written word. This isolation might be why the soul that departs the body and travels into the heavens is missing in Middle Eastern (except Egyptian) mythology.

CHINESE ASTROLOGY AND ASTRONOMY

For those desiring to get in touch with their inner feline, you can combine the Chinese Year of the Tiger with your European-type astrological sign and obtain some idea as to your spiritual future, at least for 2023 and the next ten years. The Chinese zodiac is made up of the Rat, Ox, Tiger, Rabbit, Dragon, Snake, Horse, Goat, Monkey, Rooster, Dog, and Pig. Anyone who has eaten at a Chinese restaurant has seen the traditional placemat providing the patrons a brief personality sketch and who to hang out with, or perhaps, who not to marry and who would be a better mate.

If you were born in the year 1938, 1950, 1962, 1974, 1986, 1998, 2010, or 2022 you were born in the year of the Tiger. "Tiger people are aggressive, courageous, and sensitive. Look to the horse or dog for happiness. Beware of the Monkey."*

This astrological divination procedure stems from the gods making the first calendar, wherein the first twelve animals to complete a race would be included. There are only two signs that match up with Greek mythology/astrology, the Ox and the Bull and the Goat with the Ram. The Western signs, although there are more constellations noted in astronomy, are the Ram, Bull, Twins, Crab, Lion, Virgin, Scales, Scorpion, Centaur, Sea-Goat, Water Bearer, and Fish.

The Chinese system, used for determining personality, is derived from the Five Elements: *fire* signs are inspired by excitement, *earth* signs are motivated to secure foundations, *metal* signs are driven to create order, *water* signs are compelled to form emotional bonds, and those born under the *wood* element have a desire to explore.

---

*I obtained this from a placemat at a Chinese restaurant.

The Western system only identifies four signs. *Water* signs are driven by emotion, *earth* signs are practical, *fire* signs are impulsive, and *air* signs are intellectually oriented.

The Chinese zodiac and that of the Europeans are used by many people for purposes of direction, essentially divination (or diagnosis; analysis of urine and blood are divination procedures in Western medicine; urine and blood analysis only help, like all divination procedures, to make decisions regarding medical procedures—they don't necessarily inform as to cause), as a way of determining, predicting, or mapping the future. What I find of interest is the choices that people make when asked to choose and act out an animal, sort of what transpired in one film of the *Harry Potter* series. Those who chose a feline rarely chose a domesticated cat, which suggests that part of their spiritual nature, at least to the individual, resides in power, the ferocity that kills, but also the power that protects. Domesticated house cats are not lions and tigers. For those desiring to get in touch with their inner feline, you can combine the Chinese Year of the Tiger with your European-type astrological sign and obtain some idea as to your spiritual future, at least for 2022 and the next eleven years.

The Chinese were astute astronomers, initially for divination and determining good and bad omens, often used in conjunction with oracle bones (the heating, cracking, and interpretation of a deer scapula, etc.) but they accurately cataloged supernova and comets.* Divination procedures using cosmological reference were mainly used to inform if appropriate sacrifices were made to the gods. It was only after the unification of China (c. 1500 BCE) that cosmological divination turned into what we today would call astronomy.

Naming the constellations after animals was not a practice in Chinese astronomy and, although the heavens were used for divination purposes (especially by the court), Chinese astronomy should not be confused with astrology.

---

*For those interested in Chinese astronomy, see Jiang and Chen 2021.

ANCIENT EGYPT

Astronomy in ancient Egypt can be traced back to between seven and eight thousand years ago, beginning perhaps with the calendar site at Nabta Playa in the southern part of the Western Desert (Bauval and Brophy 2011). It was probably cattle herders who built this megalithic structure, likely attempting to predict weather patterns, especially rain, as it was at this time period that global warming (not caused by sinful humans) was turning the once lush grasslands in Libya and Egypt into desert. And, if our interpretations of cat domestication are correct, the cattle herders were accompanied by cats, who not only ate mice but killed scorpions and cobras.

The pyramids were aligned according to the cardinal points of the compass, and some say the alignment of the pyramids on the Giza plateau matches Orion's belt. Not only is there controversy regarding the age of the Great Pyramid of Khufu (Creighton 2017; Bauval and Osman 2012; Bauval and Gilbert 1994), the age of the Sphinx has been brought into question as well (Schoch 2012, 10–37; Schoch and Bauval 2017). According to Schoch, a geologist, water marks on the Sphinx suggest a deluge perhaps pushing the date back at least to 7000 BCE if not 10,000 BCE:

> However, there is the distinct possibility that this analysis underestimates the age of the Sphinx. Subsurface weathering rates often proceed nonlinearly; that is, the deeper the weathering goes, the slower it progresses because of protection from the overlying material. If we assume this is the case, then the estimated date above is only a bare minimum. The possibility of nonlinear weathering suggests that the very earliest portion of the Sphinx could date to before 7000 BCE, perhaps even as early as circa 10,000 BCE.
>
> [. . .] However, Göbekli Tepe in Turkey . . . dates back to the end of the last ice age, circa 10,000 BCE to 9000 BCE, and at this

point I find it tenable that the oldest portion of the Great Sphinx may date back to this remote period as well. (Schoch 2012, 21)

Schoch (2012, 21) goes on to say:

It has been suggested that the leonine aspect of the Sphinx connects it to the constellation Leo. In terms of zodiacal precessional ages, the transition from the Age of Virgo to the Age of Leo occurred around 10,500 BCE. Is it just coincidence that, based on the geology, the Great Sphinx, with a lion's body (originally the Sphinx may have had a lion's head as well) symbolizing Leo, dates back to a very remote Period?

Although Schoch suggests caution with this interpretation, he may be correct. The consensus among Egyptologists is that the Sphinx, carved from the limestone on the Giza Plateau, was constructed at the same time as the Great Pyramid of Khufu. *But keep in mind that consensus does not mean truth.* Remember the consensus put forth by the Catholic Church that the sun revolved around the earth and what happened to those who disagreed? When consensus becomes dogmatic you no longer have scientific inquiry.

In any case, the Sphinx does represent the lion, perhaps as a gate guardian or power over the cosmos, but nonetheless a spiritual object.

DIVINATION AT HOME
WITH YOUR CAT

Tarot cards have been popular in the United States for over one hundred years, with every major tarot deck construction available by 1915. Since that time many others have been produced, all with similar symbols, but the art representing the symbols has dramatically changed (Smith, "Tarot Heritage"). More recently, however, we encounter oracle cards with fewer rules but offering similar insights.

Tarot card reading can be quite complex, with more complex interpretations offered by the tarot reader as each card is chosen. Oracle cards can be used in a similar manner but statements regarding the card drawn can be left simply to the participant, which also leads to introspection. Tarot and oracle cards serve to confront the person, in a low-risk, third-person manner. So instead of telling a person that he or she is overly aggressive or not paying proper attention to health or being inconsiderate of others, they read it in the "authority" of a card or cards. In ancient Egypt Pharaoh would exclaim "So it is written, so it shall be"—and this is the way it would be. So the cards act as third-person authority figures for exploring oneself, especially since the cards represent "ancient" knowledge and understanding of the cosmos and the human condition.

I have a *Cat Tarot* deck. It is quite attractive and is utilized in the same fashion as, for example, the *Rider-Waite Smith* deck. But if you want to specifically consider your animal nature, the oracle cards are the way to go. One such oracle deck is *The Wild Unknown Animal Spirit Guidebook*; cats (panther and lion) are found in one category, that is "fire." There are a number of ways to play this. For example, if you are having trouble deciding or getting motivated, you shuffle the deck, randomly pick a card, and read the message. If the Panther is drawn we read,

ANNIHILATION OF THE
UNNECESSARY, PURGING

The Panther won't stand to see our growth or energy stagnate. Instead, it pounces into our lives and causes all kinds of havoc [. . .] with the ultimate intention of bringing us toward more fulfilling lives. It is unexpected, uncomfortable, and sometimes feels devastating, but after all the dust clears it's easy to see the Panther's wisdom at work. We've all been through these experiences, and they've made us better people. Trust that the Panther's journey always leads to a higher place.

When in Balance; brave, productive

When out of Balance; self-destructive

To bring into Balance; get rid of the unnecessary (Krans 2018)

For the Lion we read,

PATIENT, REGAL, A COMPLETE MASTER

The Lion is the master of the Fire Element and living mascot of Self-transformation. A Lion personality dedicates their life to personal and spiritual growth. This dedication inspires some and intimidates others, therefore the Lion is respected by all but known intimately by few. Some mistake the Lion as hard to access or aloof, yet those with a keener eye know better. Lions are observant, stealthy, and precise in their words and actions. They do not waste energy or resources. This card reminds us that self-mastery is available to all, no matter where our quest begins.

When in Balance; the epitome of peace and strength

When out of Balance; withdrawn, too serious

To bring into Balance; daily meditation and friendship. (Krans 2018)

As I understand, you can randomly pick another card as a means of balancing the first pick, which can allow more insights into self and others. Also, these cards can be used in group exercises, which also can lead to interesting insights.

I have two other decks that reference animals or animal spirits, the puma in *Spirit of the Wheel: Meditation Deck*, by Linda Ewashina, and *Medicine Cards: The Discovery of Power Through the Ways of the Animals*, by Jamie Sams and David Carlson, where the mountain lion, lynx, jaguar, and panther are referenced. I see these types of divination/introspection procedures as nonthreatening and certainly less expensive than a visit to a tarot reader or psychiatrist.

CATS, SPIRITUALITY, AND
THE QUANTUM WORLD

Many of the films mentioned in chapter 6 feature both this world and the other side, with that other world possibly intersecting with our own. And, indeed, this "other side" may exist; in science one must keep an open mind as all things are possible, even though they cannot be currently measured using materialistic science (math, chemistry, and physics). Moreover, there has to be more to science, yet to be discovered, than math, chemistry, and physics. If there wasn't we would have solved the riddles of the universe by now.

The word quantum refers to a very small quantity of energy that radiates at a particular frequency; the quantum world is what our physical world rests on. Apparently, according to the theories, the universe is a waveform and it only becomes particles (rocks, water, trees, and the like) when measured (measurable using math, chemistry, and physics) or observed. In order to be observed you need a lifeform that can "separate" itself from the waveform via its senses (Lanza 2020; Hoffman 2019), senses designed to interpret the universe in ways suited to nutrient quest and reproduction. In your waking state you see these particles as trees, cats, rocks, the moon, and so on.

At the quantum level there is no time or space—everything happens at once, or so it seems. Because there is no time or space there is instant communication throughout (the reader will recognize the problems in talking about this "environment" without referencing time and space). As a weak example, you pluck a guitar string, and the total length of the string is affected, not just the part touched. In a sense, then, the waveform that is the universe is a singularity of sorts where everything and nothing is happening at once. However, in back of the waveform there has to be a set of rules or instructions for assembling the tangible world out of particles once observed, and these rules are somehow coded in the way we experience our worlds.

Where did these rules and codes come from? No one, that I am aware off, can prove the universe came about out of nothing or randomly self-assembled. Many of the chemicals necessary for life are antagonistic toward one another, and it takes large amounts of energy and timing for combinations to occur; this is where we get into the issue of thermodynamics. This is all modern metaphysics, and just because "important people" believe in self-assembling universes does not mean they are correct, and it doesn't make them wrong, even though the laws of thermodynamics inform us that self-assembly is "highly unlikely." Again, we are dealing with opinion and thus metaphysics. As I pointed out (Rush 2021b, 85–86): "In the 1960s (see Moorhead and Kaplan 1967) mathematical calculations revealed that it would be impossible for even one small functional protein to be randomly created during the age of the universe." There are some problems with the math, but in 1972, using calculations based on *equilibrium thermodynamics,* Prigogine at al. (1972, 31) concluded:

> The probability that at ordinary temperatures a macroscopic number of molecules is assembled to give rise to the highly ordered structures and to the coordinated functions characterizing living organisms is vanishingly small. The idea of spontaneous genesis of life in its present form is therefore highly improbable even on the scale of the billions of years during which prebiotic evolution occurred.

There appears to be only one connection between the particle world (the one you touch and feel) and the waveform, and that is through conscious awareness. Consciousness (like a light bulb, it is either on or off) and consequent awareness of that which surrounds us, the thoughts and dreams you experience, are, in themselves, waveforms! Dreams and thoughts don't exist as particles, at least as far as neuroscientists are concerned. It is our thoughts and dreams, waveforms in themselves, that touch the waveform that is the universe.

The most famous cat connected to quantum physics is Schrödinger's Cat, a thought experiment, where a cat in a box is both alive and dead until observed. I don't think Schrödinger liked cats too much, as he could have chosen a dog or even a person. In any case, I won't get into it in this publication, but the issue is called "superposition" where, at the quantum level, all conditions are possible until a lifeform measures or observes, in this case, what is in the box. Einstein had problems with quantum mechanics mainly because it did not abide by his theory of relativity—classical physics involves time and space, and, at the quantum level, time and space do not exist (in the classical sense), at least according to the metaphysics.

As mentioned above, when observed, for example through experimentation, the waveform collapses and particles emerge (Lanza 2020; Hoffman 2019). The chair you are sitting on, when not observed, is perhaps a swirling bunch of flickering lights. Your nervous system is constructed or programmed to interpret the environment, bring it into being, so to speak, in ways that would be useful for survival of the human animal. Just think about that for a moment; through observation you bring "things" into existence. Do our thoughts create the universe? Well, perhaps the universe was there before, but the forms it takes are a product of how your nervous system is programmed to interpret them. Your cat, as an example, interprets the world differently. In the ancient Hindu metaphysics:

Vishnu sleeps on the cosmic serpent, dreaming the dream of the universe, while Lakshmi rubs his feet, causing Vishnu's dreamtime, for, in the Hindu tradition you cannot have male energy by itself. All is there, but it isn't there as well. All of a sudden, unbeknownst to Vishnu, a lotus emerges from Vishnu's navel, the lotus blossom opens and seated atop is Brahma, who opens his eyes and a universe emerges, and after 8,640,000,000 years, Brahma closes his eyes and sinks back into Vishnu only to rise again after a long sleep.

As in the Hindu tradition, the universe is only evident when observed, and like Brahma we are all creator gods in our own way.

We enter the waveform in a number of ways and the most obvious is by thinking (you do not think in particles, and these waves can be measured). Thinking is a process of popping in and out of the waveform. Insights can come to us when we think. The question is, are these generated within, do they have another source, or is there a combination of the two? Perhaps we have missed something or our science is not up to the task. As an example, you think of someone, the phone rings, and there she is. Is this just coincidence? This has happened to me many times.

Likewise, we enter the waveform through dreaming, and it is through dreaming that we may be in touch with others who are also dreaming. Perhaps this is why we encounter unfamiliar people, places, and things in our dreams; our dreams have crossed paths. Keep in mind that when you dream you enter the waveform and leave the field of time. The Italian sorceress discussed earlier, Mae, told the story of encountering a witch in her dreams. Dream-crossing can involve soul-shifting as with the Hmong and other examples from Southeast Asia.

The waveform can be conceptualized as a "stream of life" representing the secrets of the universe or "Akashic record." We have all had experience of this, for example, when trying to solve a problem, or put a concept into words, and, stumped, decide to "sleep on it." There is a part of us that is very wise. It knows all the chemistry of food digestion, all the physics, geometry, and calculus that allow us to throw a ball or walk down the street. Your skin knows how to protect itself from the sun (to a point) through the production of melanin, and the cells know how to heal a scratch or cut. The intelligence of the cell thinks to the future and alters our genetic code accordingly. Scientists are thinking in this direction, attempting to be as smart as the cell, but are a long way from altering the genetic code to, for example, repair genes connected to diseases or stop aging. We think, make decisions, and put a person on the moon, reasoning *that* is what intelligence is all about, but that is our ego talking. Our cells and their ancestors are the genius within. All life forms, even quasi life forms like prions and viruses, operate at a level of intelligence that our conscious selves can only dream of emulating. The ancient alien hunters believe that all our knowledge, of cosmological thinking, math, and so on, was given to us by space aliens. In fact, the secrets of the universe exist within the cell and over time these secrets bubble to the surface as we "sleep on it." Don't be shy; cells will share their secrets. Ask the question, ask for an answer, and go to sleep. And, by the way, I think it an insult to humanity to suggest that all we know came from space aliens because our ancestors were just too stupid to come up with solutions to problems on their own.

From the information we have on dreaming in ancient Egypt, and knowing that some priests were paid to dream, it seems likely that they were aware that one's dreams could intersect with those of others. Certainly they could contact the gods in their dreams, or they believed they could. It is likely, as noted earlier, that temple priests, as least in Egypt, observed that cats dreamed (through twitching and so on) while in sleep mode.

In ancient Egypt, dreams could be understood as an external phenomenon—as a sort of liminal zone between the living and the divine worlds, or they could be used as literary devices (Szpakowska 2003, 2).

By "external phenomenon" is meant that these images and sounds in the dream came from *outside in*—they are generated in another "place" and then come into your mind, your place. Transferring this to the cat, if cats had dreams it must mean they were visited by the "other," including deceased cat relatives, human caretakers perhaps deceased, and the neteru or the gods and goddesses.

But what do cats dream about, and did the priests ever dream of cats? Well, we can never be sure what a cat dreams about, although it is likely similar to us in organizing or categorizing, in some manner, familiar objects and people. From Gardner's 1935 work, *The Ramesside Dream*

Book, we encounter numerous dreams and their analysis. Each dream begins with, "If a man sees (himself, some animal, object) in a dream (doing something, etc.)" (Szpakowska 2003: 86). For example: "If a man sees in a dream a large cat: good; it means that a large harvest is going to come to him" (Szpakowska 2003, 86).

The author then gives a most likely explanation, knowing Egyptian symbology: "On the surface, this seems to be a simple play on *mjw* . . . and *smtw*. . . . In addition, seeing a large cat may imply a lack of grain-eating rats therefore a large harvest. Equally likely is that this is a reference to the Great Cat, who in glosses in both Coffin Text Utterance 335 and Book of the Dead 17 is described as being the god Ra" (Szpakowska 2003).

Ancient Egyptians share with other cultures the belief that dreams were a way of communicating with individuals both living and dead:

> In numerous cultures around the world, a dream is considered to be a practical means of communication between an individual and residents of the farworld, including the dead, the deities and ancestors. In the ancient Egyptian cosmos, the farworld was thought to be populated by the dead, both justified . . . and unjustified . . . and the gods (ntr.w*). These entities, although they often remain hidden and inaccessible, nevertheless had a direct impact on the daily lives of the Egyptians. They could help the living with such mundane matters as property disputes or the birth of healthy children, as well as afflicting the living with sickness or disease. From earliest times the Egyptians exhibited a desire to contact those in the farworld through various means. (Szpakowska 2003, 123)

Dreaming and death seem to be on equal footing when it comes to communicating with the departed as well as the gods, and the connection between cats dreaming and the sacrifice and mummification of cats to

---

*ntr.w is the Egyptian word we spell *neteru*.

commune with the gods or the departed seems likely. With communication in a dream you can never be exactly sure your message was heard or the interpretation of the dream was correct. But in the metaphysics of the ancient Egyptian, who better to commune with the gods than a cat (or perhaps a hawk or crocodile). The ancient Egyptians must have believed that humans could communicate with cats and the cat would faithfully deliver their messages to the gods. This speaks volumes regarding the perceived spiritual nature of cats, that is, their otherworldly connections.

Dreams for the ancient Egyptians were not always instructive in a positive way as evidenced by nightmares. I haven't found any references to cats in bad dreams. But the fact that lions were around and occasionally ate your neighbor suggests the cat might have come up in dreams in a not so positive manner. In fact, the cat dream interpretation mentioned earlier, "If a man sees in a dream a large cat: good, it means that a large harvest is going to come to him" could just as well have a negative connotation, such as "Today you will be eaten by a large cat."

For the most part it would appear the priests rendered dreams in metaphor and in a positive light. Even today therapists who interpret behavior and dreams render them in the positive, hopefully creating a self-fulfilling prophecy. For example, if a patient reported a dream to me of falling down while walking across a river, I certainly wouldn't say, "Oh, no . . . you're going to die!" No, you spin the symbols and turn them into a positive. A good therapist has to be a good storyteller.

Before moving to cats in Chinese dreams, let me mention a common issue in dream analysis, and that is the close similarity between myth and dreams. As Freud determined, myth and dream were very similar as they "read" in a similar way and speak to us in symbols or what Jung called "archetypes." As mentioned many times above, our fear of the dark, of being eaten or mauled, is embedded in our genes, and it is not surprising that dreams will often reflect these fears with more modern symbols, including tax audits (talk about monsters!), failure on an exam, and so on. Dreams have a timeless quality to them, with disconnected people and places, some recognizable, others not so much. Familiar places are somehow unfamiliar, we try to find things or places and can't, we try to move and can't, we can fly, and so on—but the dream always seems reasonable, at least while we are having the dream. The reason for this has to do with time and distance, those issues of relativity. Once in the dream state you move from the field of time to a "universe" where time and space do not exist, at least in the way we think of them in our waking state, and while dreaming—because you are in the waveform, time and distance do not matter, and all seems normal for that "environment." Upon waking most dreams seem "strange" or "odd," because in our waking state we are controlled by time and distance as they are connected to objects and events. Relativity, that is, comparison between this and that, is the major "tool" we call upon to organize our worlds. The waveform obviously is not "organized" in that way; we do not have mathematics, chemistry, and physics to explain the "ways of the waveform" that is the universe. In the waveform there are no obstructions caused by time and space—all is Buddha consciousness.

Dreams have been important in Chinese culture for over three thousand years. In the Zhou Dynasty (1046 BCE) there was an interpreter of dreams assigned to the court, the position referred to as Tai Pu, indicating the importance of dreams in conducting affairs of state (Pei and Juwen 2000, 12). Because of the importance of dreams, one could predict that a more sophisticated process of dream analysis or interpretation would come into play compared to that encountered among the Egyptians. Over time a number of different classification systems emerged, all the way from dreams as a product of disease, anxiety, or preoccupation with a problem, to weather conditions. Dream content, however, could involve cats—domestic, as well as large cats, the lions and tigers.

Cat

A dream of a cat is a sign of impending hostilities or conflicts.

The *Chao Ye Jian Zai* tells that Xue Ji Yong, governor of the county of Ji Zhou, dreamed of a cat lying at the door of his front hall, with its face turned toward the outside. He asked the interpreter Zang Xian about the meaning of this dream and Zang pointed out that the cat has teeth and paws, used for hunting and protection. "If he lies at the door, it is intending to block dangers from without. It means that there must be an army coming." In less than ten days another official in Jui Zhou started a rebellion (Pei and Juwen 2000, 54).

The cat in the above case suggested danger, as in the film *The Matrix*, while the cat itself was not the danger nor would it engage the danger. But this interpretation points out the guardian nature of cats, just as we encountered with the ancient Egyptians.

Dreams of larger cats, however, demand a different interpretation.

Lion and Tiger

A dream of a lion or tiger portends gaining great power. The tiger is regarded as the king of mountain beasts while the lion has a magnificent mane and shows unusual strength. Dreams of lions and tigers were seen as positive omens, symbols of nobility and power. Tigers are associated with the color white and the direction west.

The *Book of the Southern Dynasties* tells a story of Jing Ze, King of Qi, who dreamed he was riding a five-colored lion. Sometime later, a new emperor came into power and Jing Ze was promoted to a high-ranking position. Another story in the *Gui Hua* tells that in the Ming Dynasty one Chen You Ding was born into an impoverished family and worked as a servant in the Luo family. One day Chen lost a goose belonging to the master of the family. In fear of punishment, he ran to the Wang family, who provided him with emotional support. Master Wang had just had a dream in which he saw a tiger sitting at his door. He awoke just as Chen arrived and so believed that his dream was an omen. He felt that he had found the "tiger at his door" and arranged the marriage of his daughter to Chen, who later became very rich (Pei and Juwen 2000, 97).

The house cat, then, is an omen indicating problems in the future. As the cat is positioned near a door, with teeth and claws, it represents a symbolic guardian. But the cat doesn't act in the *manner* of a guardian or prevent others from entering. In this sense a guardian warns of impending problems.

Lions and tiger are not so much guardians as omens of power bestowed in the future, and although there is a differentiation of meaning between the house cat and lions and tigers, we see similarities with ancient Egypt. One gets the impression that dreams among the Chinese were both created in the mind of the dreamer and, similar to ancient Egypt, enter the dreamer from *outside* in the form of omens.

Dream interpretation can be complex or straightforward.

In some Amerindian societies, the dream text is analyzed by breaking down the narrative into isolated elements that are then read as an allegory, an inversion, a wish, or else a literal description of past, present, or future occurrences in the world. Hupda Makú dreamers in Brazil, for example, reduce a dream to a symbol such as "cassava bread" or "shotgun" or else into an action such as "drinking" or "shooting a jaguar." These elements are then interpreted as either a reflection or a reversal of waking reality in terms of visual, auditory, or sensory analogs expressed as metaphors. Since cassava bread resembles the giant armadillo's armor, and the long barrel of a shotgun resembles the long snout of an anteater, a dream image of cassava bread means that the dreamer will shoot an armadillo, while the image of a shotgun indicates that he will kill an anteater. . . . Shooting a jaguar (since jaguars are shamans) indicates that the dreamer is in fact being shot with illness by a sorcerer's dart. (Tedlock 1999, 90–91)

As stated, the jaguar is an important symbol in Mexican and South American cultures and it is not surprising that dreams and interpretations would reflect the belief that shamans were jaguars, that shamans could fly and enter dreams and injure individuals when they slept.

No discussion of dreams would be complete without reference to Sigmund Freud and Carl Jung and their interpretation of cat dreams. An article entitled "11 Different Cat Dreams, Decoded" examines this: "According to Freud, cats represent erotic tension, but Jung believed cats were an archetype, a source of internal inspiration and guidance. Cats can certainly be linked to your sexual energy or be a sign that sexual adventure is on your mind or might just be on the horizon." (Peters, Cheung, and Steber 2019).

Freud was preoccupied with sex which, like fear, is a necessary ingredient of life. Although I disagree with Freud's narrative for the origin of culture and religion, fears (of not having enough food, becoming the food of others, and so on) and desires (sex and the continuation of the species—immortality) are at the base of human culture. In Hinduism and Buddhism, the way to *moksha* (in Hinduism, a release from the cycle of death and rebirth or, essentially, suffering) and *nirvana* (Buddhism) is to abandon all your fears and desires. This eliminates suffering because, essentially, you become nothing. Buddha realized you could never be rid of your fears and desires, because ridding yourself of fears and desires is a desire in and of itself and, more importantly, this is not all about you. So you take the middle path and do the best you can.

Be that as it may, we can see in the movie *Cat People* (1942) this erotic theme of living in a primal condition and losing control. Freud's work was very much in vogue during the 1930s through the 1950s, so it is not surprising to find the cat wrapped around this symbolism. Freud, interpreting the dream of the cat, in all probability, was rendering an interpretation based on encountering a female cat in heat, out in the village square, screaming and wanting company.

Jung, on the other hand, did not buy into Freud's sexual overextension or preoccupation, and saw the cat as less of a primal symbol, more in the social realm as a therapeutic device. Telling a patient that a cat equals sexual desires, a preoccupation, is simply analysis and does not help the patient move past those primal urges, if that is the goal of the therapy. Jung seems to look past the primal desires and focuses on turning those energies in another direction.

The fact that we encounter the cat in dream narratives dating from five thousand years ago to the present suggests the deep connection we have to cats, again, dating back millions of years. Cats twitch and move their paws when dreaming, and this was undoubtedly noticed by the temple priests and others. And, although the domesticated cat has been part of human culture for thousands of years, it is likely that the connection between cat dreams, the Underworld, gods, goddesses, and demons emerged slowly as our ancestors, the ancient Egyptians, for example, became more familiar with cat behavior and characteristics. The lion was a familiar and ancient icon; its power was well appreciated.

The issue of quantum mechanics and waveforms, however, suggests that dreams merge within the waveform that supports the universe. And that being the case, perhaps the ancient Egyptians were correct in the belief that the cat, in particular, could communicate with the gods and goddesses and the deceased, and messages could be sent back and forth as all ends up eventually in the waveform. Quantum physics also suggests that we can be in contact with the living through our dreams especially when dreams cross, as was the case of Mae and the witch. After all, we exist as part of the wave form (the material part) and all the secrets are there for the taking, perhaps best accessible through deep meditation, dreams, hypnosis, or mind-altering substances.

Conclusion

For millions of years we've had a hate/love relationship with cats. At first, we were their prey, day after day and night after night. In terms of endocellular selection, the fear of being eaten is etched on our genes and was a major factor in our physical and social development. Our ancient ancestors banded together and developed survival skills centering on bonding and on communication designed to warn of danger. Communication skills, over time, went from hoots and hollers to the languages we use today. Language as we know it probably developed at least three million years ago and allowed us to store information in the form of symbols that could then be passed from generation to generation, allowing the accumulation of knowledge. In fact, language likely allowed us to leave Africa and collect and store information gathered from experiences in these new environments.

FEAR AND ADAPTATION

The predators, especially the cats, were a driving force in our evolution as we adapted over time to their presence and consumption of our friends and relatives. They were adapting to us as well. Eventually, around three million years ago and through analogous thinking, we began to identify with the cats, fashioning stone tools in the likeness of predator teeth. We used these tools, emulating the scavengers, to secure needed calories during those times when fruits, berries, nuts, tubers, and so on, were in short supply. These tools led to a closer and more positive identity with the cats and other predators—we were becoming them. Initially cats were the monsters in the night but became saviors, forever changing our beliefs and likely ritual practices. Now, as in the past, we recognize and honor these monsters (both the good and the bad) by incorporating them in our narratives, myths, and homes.

Our ancient ancestors were not only participants but observers of their world, and through their observation they identified the spiritual nature of cats and the physical characteristics and behaviors we saw in ourselves, or, at the very least, admired and desired.

As we were adapting to the predators, the cats, in this case, were adapting to us, observing our behaviors including our physical abilities and limitations, knowing how to sneak up and remain motionless, to blend in with the scenery and patiently waiting for a meal; they were often successful.

Ape bipedalism emerged sometime in the late Miocene, perhaps as much as eight to ten million years ago (or even earlier). Bipedalism made our ancient ancestors seem larger than they were—a choice, no doubt, that helped to deter some predation. Nonetheless whether bipedal or quadrupedal, meat was necessary for the cat's survival, and, *Dinofelis barlowi,* an archaic leopard, dined on our bipedal Australopithecine cousins in South Africa frequently (Brain 1981).

With the thrusting and throwing spears developed between eight hundred and five hundred thousand years ago, Neanderthals and modern humans became apex predators, and although still taken as prey, such technology can turn the tables, which obviously it did. Let me add that a "whacking" stick might have been used for millions of years to protect from predators while on the ground and preceded the spears that were jabbed or thrown. I notice with our cats, both inside and outside, when I have a rake, broom, or similar object in my hands, even the domesticated cats will show caution. That caution cannot be a learned behavior in our household; we don't whack our cats. Instead this behavior is likely etched on their genes. A heavy stick can inflict a great deal of damage to a cat, as can a well-placed stone. Throwing a stone accurately requires a special shoulder joint, and I am not sure when this showed up—likely before the erectus-types of around two million years ago.

Researchers have suggested that domestication of the cat took place in at least two areas, the Levant and Egypt, as it is in these areas where we first encounter agriculture (Levant) and herding of cattle (Levant and Egypt). In order for animal domestication to take place the human agency first needs a reason for doing so. Animals used as foodstuff, fur, or protection are obvious enough. The cat, on the other side, is not so easy to justify outside of its capacity to kill and eat mice. This has led some to speculate that the cat domesticated itself. The question is why? The answer may lie in that ancient relationship of prey vs. predator and the connection between us and our ancestors as food. Although *Felis chaus, Felis silvestris lybica,* and *Felis catus* do not normally eat our kind these days, that deep epigenetic connection would push them to at least be around us, and doing so provided them food, first perhaps in the form of mice in both the agricultural setting and in cattle herding, and later in our purposefully feeding cats just to keep them around.

FOLKLORE AND MYTH

Folklore and myth paint a diverse picture of the cat, from demon and trickster to an intelligent being sympathetic toward human kind. In more current renderings of the cat we encounter Catwoman in the Batman series, who is a composite of raging Sekhmet and Bastet in her disposition. The cat has become an archetype, not as a cat etched on our genes in the Jungian sense, but an image connected to fear—fear of the night, injury, and death. The domesticated cat is perhaps a reminder of those early days, millions of years ago, when we served as their food and, of course, we still do—although we serve "ourselves" out of a can of paté or bag of kibble.

Modern movies have continued to promote the image of the cat as both devil and angel, trickster and matchmaker in the same way as we see the Celtic and Japanese imaginings. Power seems to be the main characteristic attached to cats, first the big cats, the lion, tiger, leopard, jaguar, and only later *Felis*. Cats over time have become our companions, our children, and for many people they take the place of human interaction. This is especially the case for older people whose relatives and friends are deceased and the energy required to attain new relationships becomes bound to their pets and television. COVID-19 severely curtailed social interaction, and cast members of long-running "made for TV" series, like *NCIS*, *Castle*, *Lucifer*, and so on, became the new, extended family members through "binge watching" without commercials on Netflix.

The word *cat* is a symbol and, contrary to a sign, can point in many directions at the same time. The symbol, in its own way, is like the waveform that supports the tangible universe in that it can represent many things. And, like Schrödinger's Cat, the symbol is in superposition and only becomes "tangible" within a context or situation.

For some the cat is neutral; for others it is a symbol of good, of companionship or luck, while for others the cat is evil, a demon. Regardless, most would agree that the cat symbolizes power—to do good or evil. For the less spiritually inclined, the cat is simply a cat. The cat, however, is difficult to ignore—they can be big, powerful, and ruthless and urinate on your back porch or sofa, and they can be cute, cuddly companions. If we take these general characteristics back in time we can identify our fear of cats and all that goes bump in the night. And if you look to more recent times, when we became indebted to these animals for our survival, we can appreciate the cat's dual personality. In more modern times still, we have enclosed the characteristics or symbols of power, protection, companionship, and cute and cuddly within our art forms, which will serve to honor cats in the millennia to come.

Bibliography

Aesop. 1912. *Aesop's Fables*. New York: Avenel Books, originally published mid-sixth century BCE.

Allen, James P. 2005. *The Art of Medicine in Ancient Egypt*. New Haven: Yale University Press.

Badke, David. 2004. "Commentary, Saint Epiphanius on the Physiologus, Version 4." From *Sancti Epiphani Ad Physiologum*, University of Victoria Special Collections, McPherson Library (website), September 1, 2004.

Báez-Jorge, Félix. 1988. *Los oficios de las diosas*. Xalapa: Universidad Veracruzana.

Bauval, Robert, and Thomas G. Brophy. 2011. *Black Genesis: The Prehistoric Origins of Ancient Egypt*. Rochester, Vt.: Bear & Company.

Bauval, Robert, and Adrian Gilbert. 1994. *The Orion Mystery: Unlocking the Secrets of the Pyramids*. New York: Three Rivers Press.

Bauval, Robert, and Ahmed Osman. 2012. *Breaking the Mirror of Heaven: The Conspiracy to Suppress the Voice of Ancient Egypt*. Rochester, Vt.: Bear & Company.

Behe, Michael J. 1996. *Darwin's Black Box: The Biochemical Challenge to Evolution*. New York: Free Press.

———. 2007. *The Edge of Evolution*. New York: Free Press.

Benson, Elizabeth P. 1998. "The Lord, the Ruler" in *Icons of Power: Feline Symbolism in the Americas*. Edited by Nicholas J. Saunders. London: Routledge.

Bernstein, A. 1993. *The Formation of Hell: Death and Retribution in the Ancient and Early Christian Worlds*. Ithaca, N.Y.: Cornell University Press.

Black, Jeremy A., and Anthony Green. 2014. *Gods, Demons and Symbols of Ancient Mesopotamia: An Illustrated Dictionary*. Austin: University of Texas Press.

Braakhuis, H. E. M. 1987. "Sun's Voyage to the City of the Vultures: A Classic Mayan Funerary Theme." *Zeitschrift für Ethnologie* 112, no. 2 (1987): 237–59.

Bradshaw, John W. S., Rachel A. Casey, and Sarah L. Brown. 2012. *The Behaviour of the Domestic Cat*. 2nd ed. Wallingford, UK: CABI.

Brain, C. K. 1981. *The Hunters or the Hunted? An Introduction to African Cave Taphonomy*. Chicago: University of Chicago Press.

Bryan, Cyril P., trans. (1930) 2021. *The Papyrus Ebers: Ancient Egyptian Medicine*. Reprint, Eastford, Conn.: Martino Fine Books.

California Academy of Sciences. 2010. Dikika Research Project. "Scientists Discover Oldest Evidence of Stone Tool Use and Meat-Eating Among Human Ancestors." California Academy of Sciences, August 11, 2010.

Campbell, Joseph. 1991. *The Masks of God: Occidental Mythology*. New York: Arkana/Penguin Group.

Carroll, Lewis. (1865) 1993. *Alice's Adventures in Wonderland*. Reprint, New York: Dover Publications.

Collins, Andrew. 2018. *The Cygnus Key: The Denisovan Legacy, Göbekli Tepe, and the Birth of Egypt*. Rochester, Vt.: Bear & Company.

Cook, Jill. 2017. "Ahead of the exhibition Living with gods, Jill Cook takes a closer look at one of the exhibition's key loans—the Lion Man, an incredible survival from the last Ice Age." *The British Museum*. The British Museum blog (website), October 10, 2017.

Conway, D. J. 2021. *The Mysterious Magical Cat: Mythology, Folklore, Spirits & Spells*. Woodberry, Minn.: Llewellyn Publications.

Cordy-Collins, Alana. 1998. "The Jaguar of the Backward Glance" in *Icons of Power: Feline Symbolism in the Americas*. Edited by Nicholas J. Saunders, London: Routledge.

Cornell University College of Veterinary Medicine. "A Hairy Dilemma." Cornell University College of Veterinary Medicine (website).

Creighton, Scott. 2017. *The Great Pyramid Hoax: The Conspiracy to Conceal the True History of Ancient Egypt*. Rochester, Vt.: Bear & Company.

Davies, Paul. 1983. *God and the New Physics*. New York: Simon & Schuster.

———. 2008. *The Goldilocks Enigma: Why Is the Universe Just Right for Life?* New York: Mariner Books.

Davisson, Zack. 2021. *Kaibyō: The Supernatural Cats of Japan*. 2nd ed. Portland, Ore.: Mercuria Press.

Dawkins, Richard. 2019. *Outgrowing God: A Beginner's Guide*. New York: Random House.

Department of Ancient Near Eastern Art, The Metropolitan Museum of Art. 2014. "Animals in Ancient Near Eastern Art." Metropolitan Museum of Art (website), February 2014.

Donnelly, Ignatius. 1883 (2007). *Ragnarok: The Age of Fire and Gravel*. Reprint, n.p.: The Echo Library.

Dowie, Mark. 1977. "Pinto Madness." *Mother Jones* (September/October), 1977.

Driscoll, Carlos A., Marilyn Menotti-Raymond, Alfred L. Roca, A., Karsten Hupe, Warren E. Johnson, Eli Geffen, and Eric H. Harley, et al. 2007. "The Near Eastern Origin of the Cat Domestication." *Science* 317, no. 5837. (July 27, 2007): 519–23.

Driscoll, Carlos A., Juliet Clutton-Brock, Andrew C. Kitchener, and Stephen J. O'Brien. 2009. "The Evolution of House Cats." *Scientific American* 300, no. 6. (June 1, 2009). Scientific American (website).

Dunwich, Gerina. 2000. *Your Magickal Cat: Feline Magick, Lore, and Worship*. New York: Citadel Press.

Editors of Encyclopedia Britannica. "Tammuz: Mesopotamian God." Britannica (website).

———. "Nagual: Mesoamerican Religion." Britannica (website).

Evans-Pritchard, E. E. 1940. *The Nuer: A Description of the Modes of Livelihood and Political Institutions of a Nilotic People*. New York: Oxford University Press.

Firestone, Reuven. 1999. *Jihad: The Origin of Holy War in Islam*. New York: Oxford University Press.

Forbes, Alexander Robert. (1905) 2018. *Gaelic Names: or Beasts (Mammalia), Birds, Fishes, Insects, Reptiles, etc.* Reprint, CreateSpace Independent Publishing Platform.

Foster, Michael Dylan. 2015. *The Book of Yōkai: Mysterious Creatures of Japanese Folklore*. Oakland: University of California Press.

Freidel, David, Linda Schele, and Joy Parker. 1995. *Maya Cosmos: Three Thousand Years of the Shaman Path*. New York: Quill Publications.

Frigiola, Heather. 2019. *Monsters and Mythical Creatures from Around the World*. Atglen, Pa.: Schiffer Publishing.

Gadalla, Moustafa. 2018. *Egyptian Cosmology: The Animated Universe*. Greensboro, N.C.: Tehuti Research Foundation.

———. 2002. *Egyptian Rhythm: The Heavenly Melodies*. Greensboro, N.C.: Tehuti Research Foundation.

Gardiner, Alah H., ed. 1935. *Hieratic Papyri in the British Museum, Third Series: Chester Beatty Gift*, Vol I, Text. London, UK: British Museum.

Geggel, Laura. 2018. "Ötzi the Iceman Was a Heart Attack Waiting to Happen." Live Science (website), May 30, 2018.

Germond, Philippe, and Jacques Livet. 2001. *An Egyptian Bestiary: Animals in Life and Religion in the Land of the Pharaohs*. London: Thames & Hudson.

Griffith, F., and H. Thompson. 1974. *The Leyden Papyrus: An Egyptian Magical Book*. NY: Dover Publications.

Grossinger, Richard. 2002. *Dreamtime and Thoughtforms*. Rochester, Vt.: Inner Traditions.

Gunnerson, James H. 1998. "Mountain Lions and Pueblo Shrines in the American Southwest" in *Icons of Power: Feline Symbolism in the Americas*. Edited by Nicholas J. Saunders. London: Routledge.

Gurdjieff, G. I. 1973. *Beelzebub's Tales to His Grandson*. New York: E. P. Dutton & Co.

Hamell, George R. 1998. "Long Tail: The Panther in Huron-Wyandot and Seneca Myth, Ritual, and Material Culture" in *Icons of Power: Feline Symbolism in the Americas*. Edited by Nicholas J. Saunders. London: Routledge.

Heffner, Rickye S., and Henry E. Heffner. 1985. "Hearing range of the Domestic Cat." *Hearing Research* 19, no. 1 (1985): 85–89.

Herodotus. 2017. *The Histories: Volumes I and II Complete*. Translated by G. C. Macaulay. CreateSpace Independent Publishing Platform.

Hitchens, Christopher, Richard Dawkins, Sam Harris, S., and Daniel Dennett. 2019. *The Four Horsemen: The Conversation that Sparked an Atheist Revolution*. New York: Random House.

Hodder, Ian. 2006. *The Leopard's Tale: Revealing the Mysteries at Çatalhöyük*. London: Thames & Hudson.

Hoffman, Donald. 2019. *The Case against Reality: Why Evolution Hid the Truth from Our Eyes*. New York: W. W. Norton & Company.

Humane Society of the United States. "The Cat's Meow." The Humane Society of the United States (website).

Ikram, Salima, ed. 2015. *Divine Creatures: Animal Mummies in Ancient Egypt*. Cairo: The American University in Cairo Press.

Jewish Virtual Library, quoting Encyclopedia Judaica/The Gale Group. 2008. "Lilith." The Jewish Virtual Library: A Project of AICE (website).

Jiang, X., and W. Chen. 2021. *Chinese Astrology and Astronomy: An Outside History*. Singapore: World Scientific Publishing Company.

Juergensmeyer, Mark. 2003. *Terror in the Mind of God: The Global Rise of Religious Violence*. Berkeley: University of California Press.

Kennedy, Kostya, ed. 2019. *Cats: Companions in Life*. New York: Life Magazine.

Knappert, Jan, and Elizabeth Knappert. 1992. *Pacific Mythology: An Encyclopedia of Myth and Legend*. London: Diamond Books.

Krans, Kim. 2018. *The Wild Unknown Animal Spirit Guidebook*. Box Cards/H edition. NY: HarperOne.

Krauss, Lawrence M. 2013. *A Universe from Nothing: Why There Is Something Rather Than Nothing*. New York: Atria Books.

Kurten, Björn. 1976. *The Cave Bear Story*. New York: Columbia University Press.

La Fontaine, Jean de. (1683) 1983. "The Cat and the Fox" in *A Hundred Fables of La Fontaine*, 1683. Edited by Percy J. Billinghurst. Reprint, Nashville, Tenn.: Greenwich House, 138.

Lanza, Robert, Matej Pavšič, and Bob Berman. 2020. *The Grand Biocentric Design: How Life Creates Reality*. Dallas, Tex.: BenBella Books.

Lieff, Jon. 2020. *The Secret Language of Cells: What Biological Conversations Tell Us About the Brain-Body Connection, the Future of Medicine, and Life Itself*. Dallas, Tex.: BenBella Books.

Life's Abundance, "World's Creepiest Cat Legends." Life's Abundance (website), October 19, 2018.

MacKillop, James. 1998. *Dictionary of Celtic Mythology*. New York: Oxford University Press.

Magli, Guido. 2009. *Mysteries and Discoveries of Archaeoastronomy: From Giza to Easter Island*. New York: Copernicus Books.

Manniche, Lise. 1999. *Sacred Luxuries: Fragrance, Aromatherapy and Cosmetics in Ancient Egypt*. Ithaca, New York: Cornell University Press.

Marchlewicz, E., Anderson, O., and Dolinoy, D. 2020. "Early-Life Exposures and the Epigenome: Interactions between Nutrients and the Environment." *Nutrition and Epigenetics*. Edited by E. Ho and F. Domann. NY: CRC Press.

Marshack, Alexander. 1991. *The Roots of Civilization: The Cognitive Beginnings of Man's First Art, Symbol and Notation*. New York: Moyer Bell Limited.

McIntosh, Matthew A. 2020. "Hieronymous: Saint Jerome and the Lion." Brewminate: A Bold Blend of News & Ideas (website), November 1, 2020.

McNamee, Thomas. 2017. *The Inner Life of Cats: The Science and Secrets of Our Mysterious Feline Companions*. New York: Hachette Books.

Mellaart, James. 1965. *Earliest Civilizations of the Near East.* London: Thames & Hudson.

Milbrath, Susan. 1997. "Decapitated Lunar Goddesses in Aztec Art, Myth, and Ritual." *Ancient Mesoamerica* 8, no. 2 (Fall 1997):185–206.

———. 1995. "Eclipse Imagery in Mexica Sculpture of Central Mexico." *Vistas of Astronomy* 39, no. 4 (1995): 479–502.

———. 1999. *Star Gods of the Maya: Astronomy in Art, Folklore, and Calendars.* Austin: University of Texas Press.

Miller, Mary Ellen, and Karl Taube. 1993. *An Illustrated Dictionary of the Gods and Symbols of Ancient Mexico and the Maya.* London: Thames & Hudson.

Moorhead, Paul S., and Martin M. Kaplan, eds. 1967. *Mathematical Challenges to the Neo-Darwinian Interpretation of Evolution.* Philadelphia: Wister Institute of Anatomy and Biology.

Motor Car. 2023. "Swallow Sidecar Company History." Motor Car (website).

Mowat, Farley. 1963. *Never Cry Wolf.* Toronto: McClelland and Stewart.

Mullarkey, Seamus. 2021. *The Cats of America: How Cool Cats and Bad-Ass Kitties Won the Nation's Heart.* Plaines Scribes Press, Amazon.

Nagelschneider, Mieshelle. 2013. *The Cat Whisperer.* New York: Bantam Books.

Nájera Coronado, Martha Ilia. 1995. "El temor a los eclipses entre comunidades mayas contemporaneas" in *Religion y Sociedad en el area maya.* Edited by Carmen Varela Torrecilla, Juan Luis Bonor Villarejo, and Yolanda Fernández Marquínez, bub. 3. Madrid, Spain: Sociedad Española de Estudios Mayas, Instituto de Cooperación Iberoamericana, 1995, 319–27.

Nastyuk, Elena. 2019. "Cat Symbolism in Art." Arthive (website), January 1, 2019.

National Center for Families Learning. "Why Do Cats Stretch So Much?" Wonderopolis: Where the Wonders of Learning Never Cease (website).

Nishimoto, Keisuke. 2021. *Strange Tales from Japan: 99 Chilling Stories of Yōkai, Ghosts, Demons and the Supernatural.* Translated by William Scott Wilson. Tokyo: Tuttle Publishing.

Ortiz, Ernesto. 2015. *The Akashic Records: Sacred Exploration of Your Soul's Journey Within the Wisdom of the Collective Consciousness.* Newburyport, Mass.: New Page Books.

Ovid. 2016. *Metamorphoses.* CreateSpace Independent Publishing Platform.

Page, Jake. 2008. *Do Cats Hear with Their Feet?* New York: HarperCollins.

Paoletta, Rae. 2018. "Why Cats Knead, According to Science." Inverse (website), March 3, 2018.

Pei, Fang Jing, and Juwen Zhang. 2000. *The Interpretation of Dreams in Chinese Culture*. Trumbull, Conn.: Weatherhill.

Perlmutter, Dawn. 2004. *Investigating Religious Terrorism and Ritualistic Crimes*. New York: CRC Press.

Peters, Lucia, Theresa Cheung, and Carolyn Steber. 2019. "11 Different Cat Dreams, Decoded." Bustle (website), May 23, 2019.

Prigogine, Ilya, Gregoire Nicolis, and Agnes Babloyantz. 1972. "Thermodynamics of Evolution." *Physics Today* 25, no. 11 (1972): 23–31.

Rappenglueck, Michael. 2009. "Palaeolithic Shamanistic Cosmography: How Is the Famous Rock Picture in the Shaft of the Lascaux Grotto To Be Decoded?" Art Prehistorica (website), December 2009.

Reeves, Carole. 1992. *Egyptian Medicine*. Princes Risborough, UK: Shire Publications Ltd.

Robertson, Merle Greene. 1985. *The Sculpture of Palenque: Volume II, The Early Building of the Palace*. Princeton: Princeton University Press.

Ruck, Carl A. P., Blaise Daniel Staples, José Alfredo González Celdrán, and Mark Alwin Hoffman. 2007. *The Hidden World: Survival of Pagan Shamanic Themes in European Fairytales*. Durham, N.C.: Carolina Academic Press.

Rush, John A. 1974. *Witchcraft and Sorcery: An Anthropological Perspective of the Occult*. Springfield, Ill.: Charles. C. Thomas.

———. 1996. *Clinical Anthropology: An Application of Anthropological Concepts within Clinical Settings*. Westport, Conn.: Praeger.

———. 2007. *The Twelve Gates: A Spiritual Passage through the Egyptian Books of the Dead*. Berkeley, Calif.: North Atlantic Books.

———. 2011. *The Mushroom in Christian Art: The Identity of Jesus in the Development of Christianity*. Berkeley, Calif.: North Atlantic Books.

———. ed. 2013. *Entheogens and the Development of Culture: The Anthropology and Neurobiology of Ecstatic Experience*. Berkeley, Calif.: North Atlantic Books.

———. 2020. *What Darwin and Dawkins Didn't Know: Epigenetics, Symbiosis, Hybridization, Quantum Biology, Topobiology, the Sugar Code, and the Origin of Species*. Amazon.

———. 2021a. *Cat Tales: Origins, Interactions, and Domestication of Felis catus*. Amazon.

———. 2021b. *Endocellular Selection: Evolution without Darwin*. Amazon.

———. 2022. *Jesus, Mushrooms, and the Origin of Christianity*. 2nd ed. Amazon.

———. 2023. *Magic, Myth, and Religion: The Origin of Myth and Ritual Expression.* Amazon.

Santillana, Giorgio de and Hertha von Dechend. 1969. *Hamlet's Mill: An Essay Investigating the Origins of Human Knowledge and Its Transmission Through Myth.* Boston: David R. Godine, Publisher.

Saunders, Nicholas J. 1998. "Architecture of Symbolism" in *Icons of Power: Feline Symbolism in the America.* Edited by Nicholas J. Saunders. London: Routledge.

———. ed. 1998. *Icons of Power: Feline Symbolism in the Americas.* London: Routledge.

Schoch, Robert M. 2012. *Forgotten Civilization: The Role of Solar Outbursts in Our Past and Future.* Rochester, Vt.: Inner Traditions.

Schoch, Robert M., and Robert Bauval. 2017. *Origins of the Sphinx: Celestial Guardian of Pre-Pharaonic Civilization.* Rochester, Vt.: Inner Traditions.

Schwartz, Joshua. 2014. "Are Jews a Dog People or a Cat People?" *Tablet* (website), March 12, 2014.

Serpell, James A. 2014. "Domestication and History of the Cat" in *The Domestic Cat: The Biology of Its Behavior.* 3rd edition. Edited by Dennis C. Turner and Patrick Bateson. New York: Cambridge University Press.

Shojai, Amy. 2021. "Cat Language and Signals Explained." The Spruce Pets: Vet Reviewed and Pet Approved (website), November 10, 2021.

Shubin, Neil. 2020. *Some Assembly Required: Decoding Four Billion Years of Life, from Ancient Fossils to DNA.* New York: Pantheon Books.

Shuker, Karl P. N. 2020. *Mystery Cats of the World Revisited.* San Antonio, Tex.: Anomalist Books.

Shulman, David, and Guy G. Stroumsa, eds. 1999. *Dream Cultures: Explorations in the Comparative History of Dreaming.* New York: Oxford University Press.

Smith, Sherryl E. "American Occult Tarot 1910–1960." Tarot Heritage: All About Tarot History and Historic Decks (website).

Strassberg, Richard E., ed. and trans. 2002. *A Chinese Bestiary: Strange Creatures from the Guideways through Mountains and Seas.* Berkeley: University of California Press.

Sun, Jiankun. 2021. *Fantastic Creatures of the Mountains and Seas.* Translated by Howard Goldblatt. New York: Arcade Publishing.

Sweatman, Martin. 2019. *Prehistory Decoded: A Science Odyssey Unifying Astronomy, Geochemistry and Archaeology.* Kibworth Beauchamp, UK: Troubador Publishing.

Szpakowska, Kasia. 2003. *Behind Closed Eyes: Dreams and Nightmares in Ancient Egypt.* Swansea, Wales: The Classical Press of Wales.

Taussig, Michael T. 1987. *Shamanism, Colonialism, and the Wild Man: A Study in Terror and Healing*. Chicago: University of Chicago Press.

Tavernier, Chloé, Sohail Ahmed, Katherine Albro Houpt, and Seong Chan Yeon. 2020. "Feline vocal communication." *Journal of Veterinary Science*, 21, no. 1 (January 4, 2020).

Tedlock, Barbara. 1999. "Sharing and Interpreting Dreams in Amerindian Nations" in *Dream Cultures: Explorations in the Comparative History of Dreaming*. Edited by David Shulman and Guy G. Stroumsa. New York: Oxford University Press.

Tedlock, Dennis, trans. 1996. *Popol Vuh: The Definitive Edition of the Mayan Book of the Dawn of Life and the Glories of Gods and Kings*. New York: Touchstone.

Temple Head and Neck Institute. 2018. "How Does My Voice Work?" Temple Health (website), April 11, 2018.

Thompson, John Eric Sidney. 1960. *Maya Hieroglyphic Writing: An Introduction*. 3rd ed. Norman: University of Oklahoma Press.

Thorwald, Jurgen. 1963. *Science and Secrets of Early Medicine: Egypt, Babylonia, India, China, Mexico, Peru*. New York: Harcourt, Brace & World.

Turner, Dennis, and Patrick Bateson, eds. 2014. *The Domestic Cat: The Biology of Its Behavior,* 3rd ed. New York: Cambridge University Press.

u/Historian. 2018. "Mural from the Tomb of Inherkhau, Depicting Ra in the Form of a Long-Eared Feline Slaying Apophis at the Ished Tree (Tree of Life). A Scene from the Book of the Dead. (Lower quality picture without watermark in comments). Egypt, 20th Dynasty. ~1186 to 1149 BC." Reddit, r/artefactporn, June 4, 2018.

Van Huygen, Meg. 2017. "14 Legends About Cats From Around the World." Mental Floss (website), October 3, 2017.

Vocelle, L. A. 2013. "The History of the Cat in the Middle Ages (Part 5)." The Great Cat: The Cat in History, Art and Literature (website), March 1, 2013.

Voragine, Jacobus de. 1993. *The Golden Legend: Readings on the Saints*, Vol. II. Translated by William Granger Ryan. Princeton, N.J.: Princeton University Press.

Warner, Marina. 2002. *Fantastic Metamorphoses, Other Worlds: Ways of Telling the Self.* New York: Oxford University Press.

West, John Anthony. 1993. *Serpent in the Sky: The High Wisdom of Ancient Egypt*. Wheaton, IL: Quest Books.

Westreich, Sam. 2020. "Do Cats Hold Grudges?" Medium (website), June 29, 2020.

Wilkinson, Richard H. 2003. *The Complete Gods and Goddesses of Ancient Egypt*. London: Thames & Hudson.

Index

About the Author

 John A. Rush, Ph.D., N.D., is a retired Professor of Anthropology, with specialties in information theory and human information processing, myth/symbolism, and biological anthropology. Dr. Rush is also a retired Naturopathic Doctor, with specialties in nutrition, cellular toxicity, and medical hypnotherapy. His publications include:

Witchcraft and Sorcery: An Anthropological Perspective of the Occult (1974)

The Way We Communicate (1976)

Clinical Anthropology: An Application of Anthropological Concepts within Clinical Settings (1996)

Stress and Emotional Health: Applications of Clinical Anthropology (1999)

Spiritual Tattoo: A Cultural History of Tattooing, Piercing, Scarification, Branding, and Implants (2005)

The Twelve Gates: A Spiritual Passage through the Egyptian Book of the Dead (2007)

Failed God: Fractured Myth in a Fragile World (2008)

The Mushroom in Christian Art: The Identity of Jesus in the Development of Christianity (2011)

Entheogens and the Development of Culture: The Anthropology and Neurobiology of Ecstatic Experience (2013)

What Darwin and Dawkins Didn't Know: Epigenetics, Symbiosis, Hybridization, Quantum Biology, Topobiology, the Sugar Code, and the Origin of Species (2020)

Cat Tales: Origins, Interactions, and Domestication of Felis catus (2021)

Endocellular Selection: Evolution without Darwin (2021)

Jesus, Mushrooms, and the Origin of Christianity (second edition 2023)

Magic, Myth, and Religion: The Origins of Myth and Ritual Expression (2023)

Biological Anthropology: A New Synthesis (2023)